CONVECTION OVEN COOKING

CONVECTION OVEN COOKING

Linda Verkler
and Edward Zempel

PELICAN PUBLISHING COMPANY
Gretna 2011

First Pelican edition, June 1984
Second printing, January 1999
Third printing, June 2000
Fourth printing, December 2001
Fifth printing, August 2002
Sixth printing, January 2004
Seventh printing, October 2005
Eighth printing, June 2011

Library of Congress Cataloging in Publication Data

Verkler, Linda A.
  Convection oven cooking.
  Includes index.
  1. Convection oven cookery. I. Zempel, Edward N.
II. Title.
TX840.C65V47   1984   641.5'8   83-4015
ISBN-13: 978-0-88289-377-8

Printed in the United States of America

Published by Pelican Publishing Company, Inc.
1000 Burmaster Street, Gretna, Louisiana 70053

CONTENTS

INTRODUCTION

CONVECTION OVEN COOKING is a cookbook designed especially for use with convection ovens. Although the convection oven is a relatively new appliance for cooking in the home, it has been used for years in commercial baking. Chances are that those wonderful loaves of bread from your local bakery were baked in a convection oven. The last pizza you ate in a pizza restaurant was probably prepared in a convection oven. The convection ovens used in bakeries and pizza restaurants are large commercial models. However, the principle that makes them so effective is the same as that used in the small convection ovens available for home use. This principle is the forced circulation of hot air throughout the oven chamber.

Foods are cooked in less time and at lower temperatures by the continuously circulating hot air. There is a noticeable improvement in the quality of foods cooked in convection ovens. The circulating hot air seals in the natural juices of meats and poultry. Baking in a convection oven is a particular delight. It would be difficult to achieve better breads and pastries in any other type of oven. The results are dependable and delicious. With good results assured, there is greater room for creativity and versatility. As you learn to use your convection oven, it will become invaluable to you. It will not be difficult to develop a resistance to cooking again in a conventional oven. There is an art to cooking food, and the convection oven allows you to enjoy its preparation even more.

How does a convection oven work?

Convection ovens cook in a different way from conventional ovens. In a conventional oven, hot air merely rises. In a convection oven, the hot air is constantly circulated through the oven chamber throughout the cooking process. This continuous circulation of hot air ensures that all exposed surfaces of the food are more evenly browned. It also enables you to cook at lower temperatures and in less time. This makes the convection oven more economical and efficient than the conventional oven.

What are the advantages of cooking in a convection oven?

Most convection ovens do not heat up the kitchen. The hot air is recirculated inside the oven chamber and is not discharged into the room. This feature enables you to use your convection oven and be comfortable in your kitchen—even during the warmest months of the year.

Basting is unnecessary. Of course, if you wish you can baste to add flavor. However, cooking at lower temperatures and in less time, food does not dry out as in a conventional oven.

If your oven has the capability of broiling food directly on the oven rack, you will not need to turn the food being broiled.

Do foods cook faster in convection ovens than in conventional ovens?

Generally, cooking times are reduced by about one-third. This is particularly true of meat and poultry that are roasted or broiled. The surface of the meats are quickly browned, thereby sealing in the natural juices. Cooking in less time, meats are less dry.

Most baking times are the same as the baking times in conventional ovens. However, the temperatures are almost always 70°-75° less.

Are foods in a convection oven cooked at the same temperature as would be needed in a conventional oven?

For nearly every recipe, cooking temperatures in the convection oven are lower than they would be for conventional ovens. In a few instances, the temperatures may be the same. The cooking temperatures given for the recipes in CONVECTION OVEN COOKING are recommended temperatures. They are the temperatures at which we found the food to be most flavorful. All temperatures given are degrees Fahrenheit.

Does a convection oven need to be preheated?

Preheating in most convection ovens is essential to obtaining good results while roasting and broiling. It also ensures good results in baking. Depending on your oven and the temperature you wish, the preheat time should be 5-10 minutes.

Are there different kinds of convection ovens?

All convection ovens are the same in principle. However, there are differences in model designs and sizes. There are portable, counter-top convection ovens, as well as larger, convection ovens. Besides size, the only major difference in convection ovens is the method by which foods are roasted and broiled in them.

What are the differences in roasting and broiling methods in convection ovens?

Some convection ovens are designed to roast and broil food directly on the oven rack. Others are designed to roast and broil only with the use of a broiling pan. CONVECTION OVEN COOKING recipes may be used with either type of oven. However, it is important *first* to read **ABOUT ROASTING AND BROILING.**

If I have a small, counter-top convection oven, will I need to adjust the recipe sizes?

To allow for size differences in individual oven chambers, CONVECTION OVEN COOKING recipes are designed to yield relatively small quantities. For cooking in larger convection ovens, the recipes may easily be doubled. In a few recipes, specific directions are given for doubling quantities. For most recipes, the exact pan size is given. With a few exceptions, these, too, may be changed to fit the size of your convection oven.

Is a convection oven like a microwave oven?

No. The convection oven does not cook by the use of microwaves. It cooks by the forced and continuous circulation of hot air throughout the oven chamber.

Does a convection oven require special pans or utensils?

Unlike cooking with a microwave oven, there is no need for special dishes and utensils when cooking with a convection oven. The only special requirement is to use pans small enough to allow for the free movement of the circulating air. A pan that is too large will restrict this air flow and impede the cooking process.

Can I cook frozen meats and poultry in a convection oven?

You can. However, any saving in time is generally lost. Frozen meats and poultry take approximately 50 percent longer to cook than fresh meat and poultry. The times and temperatures in CONVECTION OVEN COOKING are for *fresh* meats and poultry.

Are there any foods I will not be able to cook in a convection oven?

In a convection oven, you will be able to roast, broil, and bake almost all of the foods you may have prepared in a conventional oven. Oddly enough, brownies and similarly moist batters are sometimes difficult. Individual tastes vary, however. For some, only a very moist and heavy brownie will do. We have found the results passable, but not excellent.

Is there anything else that I will need to know when using CONVECTION OVEN COOKING?

In order to make the recipes as clear and easy as possible, we have listed the ingredients in order of their use. In several recipes, a single ingredient may be used more than once. In some of these recipes, it becomes tedious to break a single large quantity into the smaller quantities needed at each stage of the recipe. In such recipes, we have broken down the net amount into the individual amounts needed at each stage. Thus, you may find the same ingredient listed more than once. Therefore, it is important to check ingredient quantities before beginning a recipe.

Whenever baking powder is called for, we use double-acting baking powder.

If you choose, margarine may be substituted for butter in most recipes. Butter gives a richer taste, however. In a few cases, margarine cannot be substituted. This is especially true in the puff pastry recipes.

If your oven is a small counter-top model, always remember first to check the pan measurements before making your batter. Although we have adjusted the recipe quantities down, there are some recipes in which adjustments will have to be made for the smaller ovens.

In covering any dish with aluminum foil, make sure that the foil is tightly secured around the edges of the dish. If the edges are not tightly secured, the circulating air will lift up the foil, causing it to fly about.

ABOUT ROASTING AND BROILING

Not all convection ovens have the same features. Besides the variations in size and design, there is an important difference in the method of roasting and broiling. One novel feature of some convection ovens is their capability of roasting and broiling foods directly on the oven rack. In such ovens, a roasting or broiling pan is not needed.

The most visible effect of on-the-rack roasting and broiling is the even browning of meat and poultry. If a roasting pan and rack are used for roasting, the browning of the meat or poultry is often not even. If a broiling pan is used for broiling, the same is often true. The bottom of the meat or poultry will not have the same color as the top. Generally, it will be lighter.

Before undertaking any recipes involving roasting or broiling, you should *carefully read the manufacturer's instructions* regarding roasting and broiling in your convection oven.

If you can roast or broil directly on the oven rack, you should first grease the rack lightly.

Hors d'Oeuvre

BROILED SHRIMP

Firm and crunchy, these are a strong temptation. You may find yourself buying more shrimp than you need—just to ensure that your guests have enough.

24 medium shrimp
1 cup olive oil
1 tablespoon lemon juice
$^{1}/_{2}$ cup dry white wine
2 cloves garlic, crushed
$^{1}/_{2}$ teaspoon basil
$^{1}/_{2}$ teaspoon oregano

Shell and devein the shrimp, leaving on the tails. Place the shrimp in a bowl just large enough to hold them.

Mix well the olive oil, lemon juice, wine, garlic, basil, and oregano. Pour this marinade over the shrimp.

Marinate the shrimp, covered and refrigerated, for at least 6 hours.

Preheat oven to 450°.

Broil for about 5 minutes. (First read **About Roasting and Broiling**.)

Makes 24 broiled shrimp.

BAKED OYSTERS

12 oysters on the half shell
$^1/_4$ cup butter
2 tablespoons grated
   Parmesan cheese
1 clove garlic, crushed
1 teaspoon gin
Bread crumbs, finely crushed
Freshly ground black pepper

Preheat oven to 450°.

Over low heat, melt the butter in a heavy saucepan. Add the Parmesan cheese. Crush the garlic in a garlic press and add. Remove saucepan from heat. Stir in the gin.

Drain most of the liquor from the oysters.

Spoon about $1^1/_2$ teaspoon of the Parmesan sauce over each of the oysters. Sprinkle with bread crumbs. Season with a little freshly ground black pepper.

Place the oysters in a shallow pan and bake for about 4 minutes. Serve immediately.

Makes 12 baked oysters.

SAUSAGE WRAPS

For these appetizers, we prefer to use Italian sausage (or a similar highly seasoned sausage). Of course, you can skip the sausage entirely—and use about 3 ounces of very sharp Cheddar instead.

Pastry for a 9″ pie
4 ounces sausage
1 small onion, minced
6 large black olives, minced
1 egg white

Roll out the pie pastry a bit thinner than you normally would.

Preheat oven to 450°. Have ready a greased cookie sheet.

In a heavy skillet, cook the sausage. Drain all but a little grease from the skillet. Add the onion. Cook with the sausage over low heat until the onion just begins to lose its color. Add the olives and mix well. Remove from heat.

Using, perhaps, a small juice glass, cut the pastry into circles with a diameter about 2″-2¹/₂″.

Place about 1 teaspoon of the sausage mixture on each of the pastry rounds. Place the sausage mixture slightly off center. Remember that the pastries will be folded.

Fold the pastry rounds, making certain that the edges meet. Crimp tightly. Place on the greased cookie sheet.

Mix the egg white with 1 teaspoon of water. Brush each of the pastries.

Bake for about 8 minutes. The pastry should be lightly browned.

Makes about 12.

KABOBS

This marinade can be used for beef, chicken, and pork. Whichever you choose, marinate for at least 4 hours in a cool place.

MARINADE
$^1/_4$ cup soy sauce
$^1/_8$ cup vegetable oil
$^1/_4$ cup dry sherry
1 clove garlic, crushed
$^1/_2$ teaspoon vinegar
A 1"-square piece fresh
    ginger, minced

Mix all of the above ingredients in a bowl just large enough to hold the kabobs.

KABOBS

The quantities given are meant only as a guide. If you choose to mix beef, pork, and chicken, broil the pork on a separate skewer. This will allow you to cook it completely, without over-cooking the beef or chicken.

$^1/_2$ pound sirloin
or
1 chicken breast, boned and
    skinned
or
$^1/_2$ pound pork tenderloin

Cut the beef, chicken, or pork into pieces about 1" square. Each piece should be $^1/_4$"-$^1/_2$" thick.

Add the kabobs to the marinade. Marinate for about 4 hours in a cool place.

Preheat oven to 450°.

Thread the kabobs onto skewers. Don't crowd the kabobs. Leave a little space between them.

Broil beef and chicken for about 4-5 minutes. Broil pork for about 6-7 minutes.

Remove kabobs from skewers. Serve immediately. (You may want to provide the ubiquitous toothpick.)

Makes about 25 kabobs.

SWEET AND SOUR CHICKEN WINGS

These are definitely "finger food." We recommend that you cut the chicken wings at the joints. If you wish, you might discard the wing tips. We prefer to broil them.

12 chicken wings

SWEET AND SOUR
   SAUCE
$^3/_4$ cup pineapple juice
1 tablespoon soy sauce
1 tablespoon vinegar
1 teaspoon ground ginger
$^1/_8$ cup molasses
1 tablespoon cornstarch

Divide the chicken wings at the joints.

In a bowl just large enough to hold the chicken wings, mix well the pineapple juice, soy sauce, vinegar, ginger, and molasses.

Place the chicken wings in the sweet and sour sauce. Marinate, covered and refrigerated, for at least 12 hours.

Remove the chicken wings from the marinade. Reserve the marinade.

Preheat oven to 450°.

Pour the marinade into a heavy saucepan. Stir in the cornstarch over low heat. Stir constantly until sauce begins to thicken.

Dip the chicken wings into the sweet and sour sauce. Coat thoroughly.

Broil about 10 minutes. (First read **About Roasting and Broiling**.)

Makes 12 sweet and sour chicken wings.

CHEDDAR TOPS

This union of Cheddar and sauerkraut is unusual—and delicious. Any hard cheese can be used.

3 slices white bread
Butter
³/₄ cup sauerkraut, rinsed
    and drained
3 ounces sharp Cheddar,
    grated

Preheat oven to 450°.

Cut each slice of bread into four pieces of equal size. Butter each of these pieces on one side only.

Place the bread, buttered side down, on an ungreased cookie sheet. Cover each piece of bread with the sauerkraut, dividing it equally. Top with the grated cheese.

Bake for about 5 minutes.

Makes 12.

QUICHE LORRAINE

1 pie pastry
4 strips lean bacon
1 cup sour cream
$^2/_3$ cup milk
$^1/_4$ teaspoon salt
$^1/_4$ teaspoon nutmeg
$^1/_4$ teaspoon white pepper
4 eggs
$^1/_2$ cup Swiss cheese, diced

Line a 9″ pie plate with pastry and refrigerate.

Boil the bacon for about 5 minutes. Drain, and mince.

Preheat oven to 375°.

Mix the sour cream, milk, salt, nutmeg, and pepper.

Separate one egg, reserving the white. Add the remaining three eggs to the yolk of the first, and lightly beat. Add to the sour cream mixture. Mix all the ingredients until well blended.

Brush the pie pastry with the reserved egg white. Sprinkle with the bacon and cheese.

Pour the sour cream mixture over the top.

Bake for about 25 minutes, or until golden brown.

Serves 6.

BROILED STUFFED MUSHROOMS

These are, perhaps, most popular as hors d' oeuvre. If the bacon is omitted, these mushrooms are a fine accompaniment to roast chicken. We have a friend who stuffs large mushrooms and serves them as a main course.

12 medium mushrooms (cap
    diameter about 2")
2 strips lean bacon, minced
1 tablespoon butter
1 medium onion, minced
2 tablespoons chopped
    parsley
Freshly ground black pepper
1 egg
$1/3$ cup grated Parmesan
    cheese
2 tablespoons butter

Preheat oven to 450°.

Wipe the mushrooms with a damp cloth. Separate the mushroom caps from their stems. Mince the stems.

Cut the bacon into pieces about $1/4$" square.

Saute the bacon in a heavy skillet. Add 1 tablespoon butter. Add the onion and saute until it begins to lose its color.

Mix in the mushroom stems. Cook for a few minutes. Add the parsley. Season with pepper.

Beat the egg slightly and add to the mushroom mixture. Cook until mixture begins to thicken.

Add the Parmesan cheese. Stir quickly to mix well with the other ingredients.

Remove skillet from heat. Allow mushroom stuffing to cool for a few minutes.

Melt 2 tablespoons butter. Brush the mushroom caps with the melted butter.

Fill the mushroom caps with the stuffing. Place, cap side down, in a shallow ovenproof dish.

Broil about 6 minutes.

Makes 12 stuffed mushrooms.

CHEDDAR PUFFS

These are very small Cheddar cheese cookies. They are easily made—and quickly gone.

$^3/_4$ cup grated Cheddar
   cheese
$^1/_8$ cup grated Parmesan
$^1/_8$ teaspoon salt
$^1/_4$ teaspoon dry mustard
$^1/_4$ teaspoon sweet paprika
Dash cayenne pepper
$^1/_4$ cup butter, melted
$^3/_4$ cup all-purpose white
   flour, sifted

Mix well the Cheddar cheese, the Parmesan cheese, the salt, mustard, paprika, and cayenne. Add the melted butter, stirring to mix well. Add the flour a little at a time. Mix until the dough is slightly crumbly.

Preheat oven to 375°.

Lightly grease a cookie sheet.

Form the dough into small balls about 1" in diameter. Flatten each ball slightly and place on the cookie sheet.

Bake for about 10 minutes.

Makes about 25-30 Puffs.

Fish

BAKED FISH FILLETS

In some   instances, the simplest is the best. Such is the case with these baked fish fillets.

1 pound fish fillets, skinned
$1/4$ cup dry white wine
Salt
Freshly ground black pepper
Savory

Preheat oven to 325°.

Butter a baking dish. Place the fillets in the dish. Pour the wine over them. Season lightly with salt, pepper, and savory.

Bake, uncovered, for about 15 minutes.

Serves 2.

BROILED CATFISH

In the American Midwest and South, fried catfish is a common dish. This is an interesting recipe for cooking catfish another way.

Four 1-pound catfish,
   cleaned and skinned
3 tablespoons lemon juice
$1/2$ cup cornmeal
Freshly ground black pepper
$1/2$ teaspoon salt

Rub the catfish with the lemon juice.

Preheat oven to 300°.

Mix the cornmeal, pepper, and salt.

Dredge the catfish in the cornmeal mixture.

Broil the catfish for 30-35 minutes. (First read **About Roasting and Broiling**.) When done, the fish should flake easily.

Serve the catfish with the following lemon-butter sauce:

$^1/_4$ cup melted butter
1 tablespoon lemon juice

Sprinkle the lemon-butter sauce over the catfish before serving.

Serves 4.

SALMON CAKES

A 16-ounce can of salmon
1 small onion, chopped fine
1 teaspoon dill seed, crushed
$^1/_4$ teaspoon salt
$^1/_8$ teaspoon pepper
$^1/_8$ teaspoon thyme
2 eggs, beaten
$^1/_2$ cup bread crumbs

Preheat oven to 350°.

Mix well all of the ingredients. Shape into four patties of equal size. Place these in a small ovenproof dish, making sure they do not touch. Bake for 25 minutes.

Serves 4.

SALMON SOUFFLE

A 7³/₄-ounce can of salmon
3 tablespoons butter
3 tablespoons all-purpose
   flour
1 cup milk
¹/₂ teaspoon salt
¹/₈ teaspoon pepper
¹/₂ teaspoon lemon juice
¹/₄ teaspoon dry mustard
3 eggs

Preheat oven to 350°.

Drain and flake the salmon.

Over low heat, melt the butter in a heavy saucepan. Stir in the flour. Add the milk, stirring steadily. Add the salt, pepper, lemon juice, and mustard. Stir the sauce until thickened and smooth. Add the salmon. Separate the eggs and beat the yolks. Add these to the salmon mixture. Cool slightly.

Beat the egg whites with a whisk until stiff. Fold the egg whites carefully into the salmon mixture. Pour into a 1-quart, ungreased souffle dish. Bake for 35 minutes.

Serves 4.

SALMON WITH RICE AND CURRIED WHITE SAUCE

A 15-ounce can of salmon
3 cups cooked rice
1 medium onion, minced
1 cup mushrooms, chopped
    (optional)
$1/8$ teaspoon freshly ground
    black pepper

Mix the salmon, rice, onion, mushrooms, and pepper in an ovenproof casserole.

Preheat oven to 300°.

Make the following curried white sauce:

4 tablespoons butter
4 tablespoons all-purpose
    flour
1 cup milk
$1/4$ teaspoon salt
1 teaspoon curry powder

Melt the butter over low heat. Add the flour a little at a time, stirring steadily. Add the milk, stirring the sauce until it is smooth. Add salt and curry powder, mixing well. Pour this sauce over the salmon mixture. Bake, uncovered, for 35 minutes. The top should be a deep brown.

Serves 4.

TUNA CASSEROLE

In the convection oven, this casserole quickly forms a golden brown crust.

A 6½-ounce can of tuna
   (preferably water packed)
A 17-ounce can of sweet peas,
   drained
10 black olives, pitted and
   halved (optional)
2 cups cooked rice
¼ cup Parmesan cheese,
   grated
¼ teaspoon salt
⅛ teaspoon freshly ground
   black pepper

Flake the tuna. Mix in the peas, olives, rice, Parmesan, salt, and pepper. Place this mixture in a 10" x 10" x 2" ovenproof casserole.

Preheat oven to 350°.

Make the following white sauce:

2 tablespoons butter
2 tablespoons all-purpose
   flour
½ cup milk

Melt the butter in a saucepan. Add the flour, stirring it in slowly and steadily. Add the milk, stirring constantly as the sauce thickens.

Cover the tuna mixture with the white sauce. Bake for 30 minutes, or until top is golden brown.

Serves 4.

STUFFED FISH

The stuffing for this fish is slight—more for flavor than substance. There are only a few stalks of celery, some parsley, and a little basil.

A 2$\frac{1}{2}$-3 pound fish, dressed
1 teaspoon dried basil
1 cup chopped celery
$\frac{1}{2}$ cup fresh parsley
$\frac{1}{4}$ cup melted butter
1$\frac{1}{2}$ teaspoons lemon juice

Preheat oven to 300°.

Rub the inside of the fish with the dried basil. Mix the celery and parsley. Stuff the fish loosely with this mixture.

Melt the butter and stir in the lemon juice.

If you can cook the fish directly on the rack, do so. (First read **About Roasting and Broiling.**) Otherwise, place it in a lightly greased ovenproof dish.

Cook the fish for about 35 minutes, brushing occasionally with the lemon butter. The fish will be done when its flesh flakes easily.

Serves 4-6.

Meat

ROAST BEEF

Remove the roast from the refrigerator two hours before you plan on roasting it. If the roast is a standing rib roast, score it lightly. Rub the roast well with freshly ground black pepper.

Preheat oven to 450°.

Place the roast in the oven. (First read **About Roasting and Broiling**.) Roast for 10 minutes.

Reduce heat to 300°.

You will want to remove the roast from the oven about 10-15 minutes before carving it. This brief period allows the juices to settle. It also makes carving easier. Remember that roast beef continues to cook after being removed from the oven. Its internal temperature may increase as much as 20°. The roasting times and temperatures given below allow for this temperature increase during the 10-15 minute resting period.

Use the following schedule as a guide to times and temperatures. NOTE: The schedule below is for roasting a standing rib roast. For rolled roasts, add about 4-8 minutes per pound.

Rare roast beef: Roast about 15-18 minutes per pound. Remove from oven when internal temperature is 110°-120°.

Medium-rare roast beef: Roast about 19-21 minutes per pound. Remove from oven when internal temperature is 120°-130°.

Medium roast beef: Roast about 21-23 minutes per pound. Remove from oven when internal temperature is 130°-140°.

Well-done roast beef: Roast about 26-30 minutes per pound. Remove from oven when internal temperature is 150°-160°.

In roasting beef, it is important to use a meat thermometer. The above roasting times are approximate. You can ensure a greater degree of accuracy by using the roasting times as a guide and checking the meat with a meat thermometer at the desired intervals.

If possible, use a thermometer that gives an instant reading. These thermometers are not left in the meat. They are withdrawn immediately after the temperature has been obtained. In taking the temperature reading, remember to insert the thermometer into the thickest part of the meat and away from bone.

DEVILLED BEEF BONES

Devilling was a common nineteenth-century cooking technique. Essentially, it consists of coating already roasted meats with a piquant sauce. In Victorian England, the bones left from what we know as a standing rib roast were commonly devilled. This may seem a long way around to obtain bones for devilling. If you don't plan on roasting such a cut, you can use what are known as braising ribs. We have even devilled beef neck bones. With these, the expected result is not the same. The meat is scant and not tender—and the sharp edges of the bone make for perilous gnawing.

The convection oven is ideal for roasting devilled beef bones.

The movement of hot air cooks a delicious crust on the meat.

4 pounds beef bones from a
    standing rib roast (or use
    braising ribs)
4 tablespoons Worcestershire
    sauce
2 tablespoons prepared
    mustard
2 tablespoons brown sugar
2 cloves garlic, minced
1 medium onion, minced
2 teaspoons lemon juice
$\frac{1}{2}$ teaspoon salt
$\frac{1}{4}$ teaspoon freshly ground
    black pepper

Preheat oven to 450°.

Make the devilling. Mix well the Worcestershire sauce, mustard, brown sugar, garlic, onion, lemon juice, salt and pepper.

The bones must be roasted before they are devilled. If the bones have not previously been roasted, roast in a 450° oven for 20 minutes. (First read **About Roasting and Broiling**.)

Remove ribs from the oven. Place in an ovenproof dish and spoon the devilling over the ribs. Turn them, making sure that they are well coated with the devilling. Let them stand for 10 minutes.

Reduce heat to 350°.

Return the ribs to the oven. Roast for about 15 minutes.

Serves 4.

SHISH KEBAB

$^{1}/_{4}$ cup olive oil

$^{1}/_{4}$ cup soy sauce

1 clove garlic, crushed

$^{1}/_{4}$ teaspoon freshly ground
   black pepper

$^{1}/_{4}$ teaspoon thyme

$1^{1}/_{2}$ pounds sirloin tips (or
   good stew beef), cut into 1″
   cubes

3 small onions, quartered

2 small tomatoes, quartered
   (or 8 cherry tomatoes)

8 medium mushrooms,
   halved lengthwise

1 medium green pepper, cut
   into 1″ squares

2 strips bacon, cut into 1″
   pieces

Mix the olive oil, soy sauce, garlic clove, pepper, and thyme.
Add the beef, onions, tomatoes, mushrooms, and green pepper.
Cover, and refrigerate for 12 hours. Turn shish kebab
ingredients two or three times. This will ensure even coverage.
Remove from refrigerator 1 hour before needed.

Preheat oven to 450°.

Thread the beef, onions, tomatoes, mushrooms, green pepper,
and bacon onto eight metal skewers. Alternate them in some
rough sequence. Remember that you will be threading eight
skewers. Attempt to balance the various ingredients.

Broil for 9-12 minutes. (First read **About Roasting and Broiling**.)

Serves 4.

BROILED CLUB STEAKS

Club steaks, 1″ thick
Black peppercorns, cracked
   (1 teaspoon per steak)

Press the peppercorns into the steaks, using the heel of your hand. Allow steaks to rest in a cool place for 1 hour.

Preheat oven to 450°.

Broil steaks. (First read **About Roasting and Broiling**.) Broil the steaks 5 minutes for rare, 7 minutes for medium rare, and 10 minutes for well done.

HAMBURGERS

The addition of a few spices adds to the flavor of ground beef, without being overpowering.

1 pound ground chuck
$1/4$ teaspoon thyme
$1/4$ teaspoon freshly ground
   black pepper
$1/2$ teaspoon celery salt
1 teaspoon Worcestershire
   sauce

Preheat oven to 450°.

Mix well the beef, thyme, pepper, celery salt, and Worcestershire sauce. Form the ground chuck into patties. If you like truly big hamburgers, form the beef into two patties, each approximately 1″ thick. For smaller hamburgers, form the beef into four patties, each approximately ¹/₂″ thick.

Broil the hamburgers. (First read **About Roasting and Broiling.**) Broil large hamburgers 20 minutes for well-done, 15 minutes for medium-rare. Broil small hamburgers 6 minutes for well-done, 5 minutes for medium-rare.

Serves 2-4.

BROILED FLANK STEAK

Easily mastered and quickly cooked, this dish is ideal for company. It must be served rare.

A 2-pound flank steak
2 tablespoons olive oil
2 tablespoons dry sherry
2 tablespoons soy sauce
2 teaspoons lemon juice
¹/₈ teaspoon freshly ground
　　black pepper
¹/₄ teaspoon thyme
1 clove garlic, minced

Score the flank steak, if this has not been done.

In a flat dish just large enough to hold the flank steak, mix the olive oil, sherry, soy sauce, lemon juice, pepper, thyme, and garlic. Place the flank steak in this marinade. Spoon some of the marinade over the flank steak. Marinate the meat, covered and refrigerated, for 12 hours, turning two or three times. Remove meat from refrigerator 30 minutes before you plan on broiling it.

Preheat oven to 450°.

Remove meat from marinade. Broil for about 7 minutes. (First read **About Roasting and Broiling**.) The flank steak must be rare. (Flank steak that is well done will be tough.) Cut on the diagonal at a 30° angle (across the grain of the meat). Slice thin.

Serves 4.

STUFFED FLANK STEAK

A 2- to 3-pound flank steak
$^1/_4$ teaspoon salt
$^1/_4$ teaspoon freshly ground
   black pepper
1 tablespoon all-purpose
   flour
1 teaspoon Worcestershire
   sauce
1 tablespoon butter
1 medium onion, chopped
$^1/_2$ cup celery, chopped
$^1/_2$ cup dried bread crumbs
$^1/_4$ teaspoon thyme
$^1/_2$ cup dry red wine
1 clove garlic, crushed

Score the flank steak, if this has not been done. Season one side of the flank steak with salt and pepper. Rub the flour into this side. Add the Worcestershire sauce, rubbing this well into the meat.

Preheat oven to 300°.

Cook the onion in the butter until it begins to lose its color. Mix the onion with the celery, bread crumbs, and thyme. Spread this mixture over the seasoned side of the flank steak.

Roll the steak as if you were rolling a jelly roll. Start at the narrow end. Tie with preshrunk string at short intervals. You might also want to run one string around both ends.

Place steak in casserole. Pour the wine over the meat. Rub the garlic well into the meat. Season with a little freshly ground pepper. Cover and cook for 1 hour 40 minutes.

Serves 4.

MEAT LOAF

1 pound ground beef
$^1/_2$ medium green pepper,
    chopped
1 small onion, minced
$^1/_4$ cup bread crumbs
1 egg, slightly beaten
1 teaspoon Worchestershire
    sauce
$^1/_2$ teaspoon thyme
$^1/_4$ teaspoon freshly ground
    black pepper
$^1/_2$ teaspoon celery salt
1 tablespoon catsup
1 slice bacon

Preheat oven to 325°.

Mix well all of the ingredients except the bacon.

Shape the meat mixture into a loaf. Place the loaf in the center of a 9″ pie plate. Place the slice of bacon on top of the meat loaf.

Bake for about 50 minutes.

Serves 4.

BEEF POT ROAST

We have always cooked this pot roast in a heavy cast-iron skillet. However, any heavy casserole can be used. In cooking, this pot roast has a very scented and rich aroma.

1¼ cups dry red wine
½ teaspoon thyme
¼ teaspoon freshly ground
   pepper
1 clove garlic, minced
6 peppercorns
1 bay leaf, crumbled
1 medium onion, sliced thin
1 tablespoon olive oil
A 3-pound boneless chuck
   roast
1 tablespoon bacon fat

In a flat dish large enough to hold the meat, combine the wine, thyme, pepper, garlic, peppercorns, bay leaf, onion, and olive oil. Mix well. Place the beef in this marinade. Marinate the beef, covered and refrigerated, for 12 hours. Turn once or twice.

Preheat oven to 325°.

Remove meat from marinade. Strain the marinade and reserve.

In a heavy skillet, heat the bacon fat. Dry the beef and brown it quickly in the bacon fat. Remove the skillet from the heat. Add the strained marinade. Cover tighly and cook for 2½ hours.

Serves 6.

BEEF BURGUNDY

If marinated beforehand, the beef will need only one hour in the oven.

1 pound of stew beef,
   trimmed of fat
1 cup dry red wine
2 teaspoons bacon fat
1 large onion, chopped
2 cloves garlic, chopped
¼ teaspoon thyme
4 juniper berries
¼ teaspoon salt
Freshly ground black pepper

Place the beef in the wine. Marinate, covered and refrigerated, for 1-2 days, mixing occasionally. Heat the bacon fat in a large, heavy skillet. In this, saute the onion until it loses its color.

Remove the stew beef from the marinade. Reserve the marinade, adding more wine, if necessary, to make 1 cup. Dry the stew beef and place it in the skillet. Saute the beef until it begins to color, turning as needed.

Preheat oven to 325°.

Remove skillet from heat. Add the marinade, garlic cloves, thyme, juniper berries, salt, and pepper to the beef and onions. Cover the skillet tightly. Cook for 1 hour.

Serves 3.

BEEF WITH BEER

Formerly, we made this dish entirely on top of the stove. The use of the oven improves the flavor of the sauce and makes a thicker gravy. The stew also needs less watching.

1½ tablespoons bacon grease
2 pounds stew beef, trimmed
    of fat
3 medium onions, chopped
1 tablespoon all-purpose
    flour
¼ teaspoon thyme
Freshly ground black pepper
¼ teaspoon salt
8 ounces beer

Preheat oven to 325°.

In a heavy skillet, heat the bacon grease and add the stew beef. Brown the meat. Add the onions and stir briefly until they are heated through. Stir in the flour. Add the thyme, pepper, salt, and beer, stirring all the time over low heat. Bring to a boil.

Cover the skillet tightly and place in the oven. Cook for 1½ hours.

Serves 4.

BEEF WITH GREEN PEPPER

We say "a green pepper," but if you like them, you might add another. We've also made it with a tomato or two. It's a good end-of-the-summer stew. And, it's easily made in the convection oven, since the oven doesn't heat up the kitchen.

2 pounds stew beef
1 large onion, chopped
1 medium green pepper,
   chopped
2 stalks celery, chopped
1 large tomato, chopped
$^1/_2$ cup dry red wine
$^1/_4$ teaspoon thyme
$^1/_2$ tablespoon salt
Freshly ground black pepper
1 clove garlic, minced.

Preheat oven to 325°.

Place all ingredients in a casserole, preferably one with a tight-fitting cover. Mix well. Cook for 1$^1/_2$ hours.

Serves 4.

GOULASH

Goulash derives its characteristic flavor from paprika. Basically, there are two varieties of paprika—sweet and hot. Most American brands seem to be sweet. If you are using hot imported paprika, 1 teaspoon should probably be enough. You can always adjust the flavor later. If using the sweet imported paprika (or most American brands of paprika), 1 tablespoon should be adequate.

2 pounds stew beef, trimmed
   of fat
1 medium onion, sliced
6 ounces tomato paste
1 cup dry red wine
2 cloves garlic, split
$^1/_2$ teaspoon caraway seeds
   (optional)
1 tablespoon sweet paprika or
   1 teaspoon hot paprika
$^1/_4$ teaspoon lemon juice
$^1/_2$ medium green pepper,
   chopped (optional)
$^1/_4$ cup sour cream

Preheat oven to 450°.

Place the stew beef in the casserole in one layer, if possible. The beef will probably have a small amount of fat in it. So, you should not need to grease the casserole. Bake uncovered, for 10 minutes. The meat should then be well browned.

In a saucepan, mix the onion, tomato paste, wine, garlic, caraway seeds, paprika, lemon juice, and green pepper. Cook over low heat for 10 minutes.

Remove meat from oven and reduce heat to 325°. Pour sauce over the meat and mix well. Place a tight-fitting cover on the casserole. Cook for 40 minutes.

Remove casserole from oven and add the sour cream, mixing it well into the sauce. Serve the goulash with noodles.

Serves 4.

CHIPPED BEEF WITH RICE AND GREEN PEPPER

This makes a tasty dish. It is a good use for a form of beef that is only beginning to win its way back from a bad reputation.

4 ounces chipped beef,
   shredded
1 medium green pepper,
   chopped
3 cups cooked rice
1 medium onion, chopped

Mix chipped beef, green pepper, rice, and onion. Place in a casserole, spreading evenly.

Make the following white sauce:

2 tablespoons butter
2 tablespoons all-purpose
   flour
$1/2$ cup milk
1 teaspoon Dijon-type
   mustard

Preheat oven to 300°.

Melt the butter over low heat. Stir in the flour slowly and steadily. Add the milk and stir until thick. Stir in the mustard.

Top the casserole with the sauce. Bake, uncovered, for 35 minutes.

Serves 4.

ONE REUBEN SANDWICH

This recipe is for one basic Reuben sandwich. Ingredient quantities may vary, depending on taste. Also, it's unlikely you will find yourself making only one Reuben. Several can be done at one time on a baking sheet.

Butter
2 slices rye bread
1 slice corned beef
3 tablespoons sauerkraut,
   rinsed and drained
1 slice Swiss cheese

Preheat oven to 450°.

Butter each slice of bread on one side only.

Place one slice of bread, buttered side down, on an ungreased baking sheet. Cover with the corned beef, sauerkraut, and Swiss cheese, in that order. Top with the remaining slice of bread, buttered side up.

Bake for about 5 minutes. Turn the sandwiches. Bake for about 5 minutes on the other side.

Makes 1 sandwich.

STEAK AND OYSTER PIE

There are several variations on this pie. The oysters are optional. If you choose not to use them, increase the amount of stew beef by one-half pound. Alternatively, in place of the oysters, you might want to use one-half pound of beef kidney, cut into small pieces. The basic recipe follows.

1 pound lean stew beef, cut
    into 1″ cubes
2 tablespoons all-purpose
    flour
¹/₄ teaspoon freshly ground
    pepper
¹/₄ teaspoon thyme
¹/₄ teaspoon salt
1 medium onion, chopped
1 clove garlic, minced
1 strip of bacon, cut into ¹/₄″
    strips
8 medium mushrooms, sliced
An 8-ounce can of oysters,
    drained (optional)
1¹/₂ cups beef stock or dry red
    wine
Pie pastry for a 9″ pie
1 egg white, or a little cream

Preheat oven to 325°.

Toss the beef in the flour. Place beef in a deep 9″ pie plate. Add the spices, onion, garlic, bacon, mushrooms, and oysters. Pour in the beef stock or wine, mixing well. The dish should be about three-quarters full.

Roll out the pie pastry a bit thicker than you normally would.

Cover the top of the dish with the pie pastry. Crimp the edges tightly. Pierce the pastry with a knife in several places. Brush with the white of an egg or a little cream. Bake for 1 hour and 20 minutes.

Serves 4.

CORNISH PASTIES

You might not think of these as fare for formal dinners, but they're excellent in "brown-bagged" lunches.

1 pound round steak
Pie pastry for a 9″ pie, rolled
   thin
1 cup potatoes, cubed
1 small onion, chopped
1 medium carrot, sliced thin
2 teaspoons butter
Salt
Freshly ground black pepper
Thyme
Cream

Preheat oven to 450°.

Cut the round steak into small cubes about ¼″ square.

Roll out the pastry a little thinner than you normally would. Using a 6″ saucer, cut four circles from the pastry.

Dividing the ingredients equally, place some of the steak,

potatoes, onions, and carrots on each circle. Add ¹/₂ teaspoon butter. The ingredients should be placed slightly off center on each of the pastry rounds. Season with salt, pepper, and thyme.

Fold the uncovered half of the pastry over the ingredients. Make sure that the edges meet.

Moisten the edges of the pastry with a little water. Crimp well, using the tines of a fork or a pastry crimper. Brush lightly with cream.

Place on an ungreased cookie sheet and bake for 10 minutes.

Reduce heat to 375°. Bake for about 40 minutes.

Serves 4.

BONED PORK LOIN ROAST

The use of a low roasting temperature (300°) ensures a moist roast.

A 3-pound boned loin of pork
1 clove garlic, halved
¹/₄ teaspoon thyme
¹/₄ teaspoon salt
¹/₄ teaspoon freshly ground
    black pepper

Remove the roast from the refrigerator 1 hour before roasting.

Preheat oven to 300°.

Rub roast with the cut clove of garlic. Season with thyme, salt, and pepper, rubbing them well into the meat. Roast for about

1¹/₂ hours. (First read **About Roasting and Broiling**.) The meat must have an internal temperature of at least 170°.

Serves 5.

BARBECUED PORK RIBS

There are three different oven settings for this dish. However, the total cooking time is only 1 hour.

4 pounds pork spare ribs
Salt and pepper to taste

SAUCE
1 tablespoon butter
1 small onion, chopped
1 teaspoon brown sugar
2 teaspoons vinegar
4 teaspoons lemon juice
²/₃ cup catsup
3 teaspoons Worcestershire
    sauce
¹/₂ teaspoon prepared
    mustard
1 teaspoon chili powder

Preheat oven to 450°.

Rub ribs well with salt and pepper. Place in uncovered pan. Place ribs as far apart as possible, trying not to pile them one on top of the other. Bake for 25 minutes.

In a heavy skillet, melt the butter over low heat. Add the onions and saute until nearly transparent. Mix the brown sugar, vinegar, lemon juice, catsup, Worcestershire sauce, mustard, and chili powder. Add this mixture to the onions. Cook over low heat 10 minutes, stirring frequently.

Reduce heat to 350°. Remove the dish and drain the grease. Add ¹/₄ cup water and cover. Return to oven and cook for 10 minutes.

Reduce heat to 325°. Remove the ribs and spread with the sauce. Bake, uncovered, for 25 minutes.

Serves 4.

STUFFED PORK TENDERLOIN

The stuffing for this is unusual, in that it consists only of onion. In fact, the stuffing might be described as a reduced onion soup. This dish is a delight.

1 cup beef bouillon
1 large onion, chopped
1 clove garlic, crushed
¹/₄ teaspoon thyme
Freshly ground black pepper
A 1¹/₄-to 2-pound pork
   tenderloin

Into a heavy skillet, pour the beef bouillon. Add the onion, garlic, and thyme. Simmer, covered, for about 15 minutes. Season with pepper. Uncover skillet for the last few minutes. Briefly increase heat to reduce the bouillon.

Cut a pocket lengthwise in the tenderloin.

Preheat oven to 300°.

Using a slotted spoon, remove the onion-garlic mixture from the bouillon.

Place the onion stuffing in the pocket in the tenderloin, distributing it evenly. Close the pocket, using skewers and string, or a needle and thread.

Broil for about 40 minutes per pound. (First read **About Roasting and Broiling**.)

Serves 4-6.

BROILED PORK CHOPS WITH DILL

8 loin pork chops,
    approximately $^5/_8''$ thick
$^1/_4$　teaspoon freshly ground
    black pepper
1 teaspoon crushed dill seed
$1^1/_2$ tablespoons olive oil

Preheat oven to 450°.

Rub the pork chops well with the pepper, dill seed, and olive oil. Broil for 8-10 minutes, or until cooked through. (First read **About Roasting and Broiling.**)

Serves 4.

LEG OF LAMB

A 5-pound leg of lamb,
    trimmed
Salt
Freshly ground black pepper
1 teaspoon thyme or
    rosemary
2 cloves garlic, sliced

Preheat oven to 300°.

Remove the lamb from the refrigerator about 2 hours before you plan on roasting it. Make small slits in the lamb. Insert a sliver of garlic clove in each slit. Rub the lamb well with salt, pepper, and thyme or rosemary.

Roast the lamb, using the following schedule as a guide. (First read **About Roasting and Broiling**.)

Rare lamb: Roast about 12-15 minutes per pound. The internal temperature should be 130°-140°.
Medium lamb: Roast about 20-25 minutes per pound. The internal temperature should be 160°.
Well-done lamb: Roast about 30 minutes per pound. The internal temperature should be 175°.

Throughout the roasting process, it is helpful to use a meat thermometer. If possible, use one that gives an instant reading.

Let the lamb stand about 20 minutes before carving.

Serves 6.

LINDA'S LASAGNE

The addition of sliced tomatoes to the sauce gives this favorite a slightly different texture.

12 lasagne noodles
1 pound ground chuck
2 cloves garlic, minced
6 ounces tomato paste
6 ounces water
$^1/_2$ teaspoon dried oregano
$^1/_4$ teaspoon thyme
$^3/_4$ teaspoon salt
1 tablespoon olive oil
12 ounces ricotta or cottage
    cheese
3 medium tomatoes, sliced
8 ounces mozzarella cheese,
    diced
2 ounces grated Parmesan
    cheese

Bring a large quantity (5-7 quarts) of lightly salted water to a boil. Gradually add the lasagne noodles. Cook until tender. This should take about 10-15 minutes. Drain the noodles when they have cooked sufficiently.

While the noodles are cooking, brown the ground chuck in a heavy skillet. Add the garlic cloves. Cook the beef and the garlic together for a few minutes. Drain any grease from the skillet.

In a small heavy saucepan, mix the tomato paste and the water over low heat. Add the oregano, thyme, and $^1/_2$ teaspoon salt. Cook for 5 minutes, stirring frequently.

Preheat the oven to 375°.

Assemble the lasagne in this way:

1. Coat the bottom and sides of the casserole with the olive oil. Cover casserole tightly.

2. Place 4 lasagne noodles side by side in the bottom of the casserole.

3. Cover the noodles with approximately one-half of each of the following, in this order:

-Tomato sauce

-Ground beef

-Ricotta or cottage cheese

-Sliced tomatoes

-Mozzarella

4. Top this first layer with 4 lasagne noodles. Lay these in a direction opposite to the noodles in the first layer. Add two-thirds of the remaining tomato sauce, and all of the remaining ground beef mixture, riccota or cottage cheese, sliced tomatoes, and mozzarella.

5. Add the remaining 4 lasagne noodles.

6. Spoon the remaining tomato sauce over the noodles, spreading evenly.

7. Sprinkle with the grated Parmesan cheese.

Cover casserole tightly.

Cook, covered, for 30 minutes.

Reduce oven temperature to 300°.

Uncover casserole. Bake, uncovered, for about 25 minutes. The lasagne should have a golden-brown crust. Allow to rest for 10 minutes before serving.

Serves 6 (4 generously).

MOUSSAKA

In making moussaka, we had wearied of feeding more and more olive oil into the skillet. We happened on this version by using uncooked eggplant. The result was excellent. Use a smaller eggplant than you usually would—and slice it a bit thinner.

1 pound ground beef or
   ground lamb
2 medium onions, chopped
6 ounces tomato paste
1 clove garlic, crushed
$^1/_4$ teaspoon cinnamon
$^1/_4$ teaspoon salt
$^1/_8$ teaspoon pepper
$^1/_2$ cup dry red wine
1 medium eggplant, sliced
   lengthwise
1 tablespoon olive oil
$^1/_4$ cup Parmesan cheese,
   grated

Brown the ground beef or lamb. Drain off all but a tablespoon of the grease. Add the chopped onions and cook slowly until the onions begin to be transparent. Add the tomato paste, garlic clove, cinnamon, salt, pepper, and wine. Simmer slowly, mixing well until flavors are blended.

CHEESE SAUCE
4 tablespoons butter
4 tablespoons all-purpose
    flour
1 cup milk
2 eggs, beaten
1 cup ricotta cheese or
    cottage cheese
$1/4$ teaspoon nutmeg

Melt the butter over low heat. Gradually add the flour, mixing well. Scald the milk and stir slowly and steadily into the butter-flour mixture. Remove from the heat. Add the beaten eggs, the ricotta cheese or cottage cheese, and the nutmeg.

Preheat oven to 350°.

Peel the eggplant. Slice lengthwise into moderately thin slices. Lightly grease a 10″ x 10″ x 2″ casserole with the olive oil. Cover bottom of casserole with one layer of eggplant. Cover eggplant with meat sauce. Sprinkle with one-third of the Parmesan cheese. Arrange another layer of eggplant. Spread this with meat sauce and sprinkle with one-third of the Parmesan cheese. Arrange a final layer of eggplant slices. Spread this top layer with the cheese sauce. You may want to pry up one or two of the top slices of the eggplant so that the cheese sauce can seep down. Sprinkle the remainder of the Parmesan cheese over the top of the cheese sauce.

Bake, uncovered, for about 50 minutes. After removing from the oven, allow the moussaka to cool for 20 minutes before serving. This allows the flavors to blend. It also gives a firmer consistency to the portions served.

Serves 6.

PIZZA

The convection oven is ideal for making pizza. The ovens in most bakeries and pizza restaurants are convection ovens. For this pizza, you may wish to vary the sauce and topping ingredients. For the dough, use the following recipe.

DOUGH
$^{1}/_{2}$ package yeast
$2^{1}/_{2}$ ounces (a little over $^{1}/_{4}$
    cup) warm water
1 tablespoon olive oil
$^{1}/_{8}$ cup milk
$^{1}/_{4}$ teaspoon salt
1 cup all-purpose flour
$^{1}/_{4}$ cup soy flour
2 teaspoons olive oil

Dissolve yeast in warm water. Into a medium bowl, place 1 tablespoon olive oil, the milk, and the salt. Add the yeast mixture when it is ready. Mix the flours and stir in. Turn out onto a lightly floured board. Knead until smooth and elastic. Add more flour if dough is sticky.

Place dough in a lightly greased bowl. Turn it so that all sides are greased. This will prevent a crust from forming. Cover the bowl with a towel and place in a warm spot to rise for $1^{1}/_{2}$ hours, or until doubled in size. When the dough has only 30 minutes left to rise, make the following sauce.

SAUCE
6 ounces tomato paste
3 ounces water
$\frac{1}{2}$ tablespoon oregano
$\frac{1}{2}$ tablespoon basil
$\frac{1}{4}$ teaspoon salt

Mix the tomato paste, water, oregano, basil, and salt over low heat. As the sauce is cooking, prepare the topping ingredients.

TOPPING
1 pound bulk Italian sausage
1 medium onion, chopped
1 medium green pepper,
    chopped
8 ounces mozzarella cheese,
    chopped fine

Brown the sausage. Drain grease from skillet. Add the onion and cook for a minute or two over low heat.

Preheat oven to 400°.

Punch down the dough. Roll out to a thickness of $\frac{1}{8}$". Fold, and roll again. Place dough on an 11" x 15" pizza pan. Prick well with a fork. Brush with 2 teaspoons olive oil. Bake for 12 minutes. Remove pizza crust from oven.

Reduce heat to 375°.

Spread the tomato sauce evenly over the pizza crust. Distribute the sausage and onions, pepper, and cheese evenly over the sauce. Bake about 25 minutes, or until the cheese is evenly browned.

Serves 4.

Poultry

ROAST CHICKEN

This low-temperature roasting method gives the chicken a delicious crust. This is the recipe for roasting a 4-pound chicken. If your chicken is larger or smaller, you can still follow this recipe. After the initial roasting period of 10 minutes at 450°, roast the chicken at 325° for about 15 minutes per pound.

A 4-pound roasting chicken
2 teaspoons lemon juice
1 teaspoon thyme
$1/4$ teaspoon tarragon
Freshly ground black pepper
$1/4$ teaspoon salt
1 small onion, peeled and
    quartered
1 tablespoon olive oil

Sprinkle 1 teaspoon of lemon juice inside the chicken. Add the thyme, tarragon, pepper, and salt. Add the onion.

Truss the chicken.

Mix 1 teaspoon of lemon juice with the olive oil. Rub the chicken with this mixture. Season the chicken with a few grindings of black pepper.

Roast the chicken breast side up at 450° for 10 minutes. (First read **About Roasting and Broiling**.)

Reduce heat to 325°. Roast for 1 hour.

Serves 4.

SHERRIED SPLIT BROILER

This chicken is first placed in a simple marinade of sherry, soy sauce, and olive oil. In just a short time, the marinade gives the chicken an unusual flavor—and contributes to its delicious crust. It can be quickly done, and serves two perfectly. All that is needed is a green salad to accompany it.

$^{1}/_{4}$ cup dry sherry
$^{1}/_{4}$ cup soy sauce
1 teaspoon olive oil
A 2$^{1}/_{2}$-pound broiling
   chicken, split

Mix the sherry, soy sauce, and olive oil in a flat dish large enough to hold the chicken. Marinate the chicken, covered, for 2 hours in a cool place. Turn once or twice.

Preheat oven to 450°.

Broil chicken for about 30 minutes. (First read **About Roasting and Broiling.**)

Reduce heat to 375°.

Continue to broil chicken for about 10 minutes per pound.

Serves 2.

DEVILLED CHICKEN

You need not confine devilling to beef bones. Devilling is an interesting way to use leftover roast or broiled chicken.

Devilling sauce for one 2¹/₂-pound broiler:

1 clove garlic, mashed
2 tablespoons prepared
　 mustard
2 tablespoons wine vinegar

Mix well the garlic, mustard, and vinegar. Remove the garlic clove.

Cut the chicken into serving pieces. Coat the chicken evenly all over with the devilling sauce.

Preheat oven to 350°.

Roast the chicken for about 15 minutes. (First read **About Roasting and Broiling.**)

Serves 2 generously.

CHICKEN WITH CHUTNEY

The use of small fryers makes a very tender dish.

1 cup orange juice
¹/₂ cup seedless raisins
¹/₄ cup chutney, chopped
¹/₂ teaspoon cinnamon
¹/₂ teaspoon curry powder
Two 2-pound fryers, cut up
¹/₂ teaspoon salt
¹/₂ teaspoon pepper

Preheat oven to 400°.

Mix orange juice, raisins, chutney, cinnamon, and curry powder. Place chicken in casserole. Season with salt and pepper. Bake for 25 minutes.

Remove chicken from oven. Reduce heat to 250°. Cover chicken with sauce. Bake uncovered, basting frequently, for 1 hour.

Serves 4.

CHICKEN WITH HERBS

We have come to think of this as a summer dish. If you have fresh tomatoes, cut them into small pieces and use them (with their juice) in place of the canned tomatoes.

A 3$\frac{1}{2}$-pound chicken, cut
   into serving pieces
2 tablespoons olive oil
$\frac{1}{2}$ teaspoon garlic salt
$\frac{1}{4}$ teaspoon freshly ground
   pepper
1 tablespoon oregano
1 teaspoon basil
1 tablespoon lemon juice
A 1-pound can tomatoes,
   drained (or an equivalent
   amount of fresh tomatoes)

Preheat oven to 450°.

Rub chicken pieces first with olive oil, then with garlic salt, pepper, 2 teaspoons of oregano, and the basil. Place chicken skin-side-up in an ovenproof casserole. Sprinkle with lemon juice. Bake for 20 minutes. Remove chicken from oven.

Reduce heat to 350°.

Cut the drained tomatoes into small pieces. Add the tomatoes to the chicken, spreading evenly over the top. Sprinkle with 1 teaspoon oregano.

Return the chicken to the oven and bake for 20 minutes. The chicken should be done when the tomatoes begin to brown on the top.

Serves 4.

HONEY CHICKEN

2 teaspoons butter
$1/4$ cup honey
$1/8$ cup prepared mustard
$1/2$ teaspoon salt
1 teaspoon curry powder
A 3-pound broiler, cut into
    serving pieces
1 tablespoon soy sauce
Freshly ground black pepper

Preheat oven to 350°.

Melt the butter. Mix in the honey, mustard, salt, and curry powder. Dry the chicken and roll it in the above mixture. Place the chicken in a casserole and pour the remaining sauce over it. Sprinkle chicken with soy sauce. Season with pepper. Bake for 35 minutes.

Serves 4.

OVEN-FRIED CHICKEN

The use of Parmesan cheese in this recipe may not be orthodox. It does, however, contribute to the flavor of the fine crust.

$1/4$ cup butter
1 garlic clove, minced
1 teaspoon oregano
$1/2$ teaspoon thyme
$1/8$ teaspoon freshly ground
    black pepper
1 cup bread crumbs
$1/4$ cup Parmesan cheese,
    grated
A $2^1/2$-pound chicken, cut
    into serving pieces

Preheat oven to 300°.

Melt butter. Add the garlic, oregano, thyme, and pepper. Mix the bread crumbs and Parmesan cheese.

Dip the chicken pieces into the butter mixture. Then dip the chicken into the bread crumb-Parmesan mixture. Place chicken in a shallow baking dish. If any of the bread crumb-Parmesan mixture is left, sprinkle it over the chicken. Bake for 50 minutes.

Serves 2 generously.

BARBECUED CHICKEN

A 3½-pound chicken, cut
   into serving pieces
1 tablespoon olive oil
1 tablespoon butter
1 small onion, chopped
1 teaspoon brown sugar
2 teaspoons vinegar
4 teaspoons lemon juice
⅔ cup catsup
3 teaspoons Worcestershire
   sauce
½ teaspoon prepared
   mustard
1 teaspoon chili powder

Preheat oven to 350°.

Place the chicken in a baking dish and sprinkle with olive oil.
Bake, uncovered, for 20 minutes.

Melt the butter in a heavy skillet. Add the onion and saute until
it begins to lose its color. Add the brown sugar, vinegar, lemon
juice, catsup, Worcestershire sauce, mustard, and chili powder.
Stir to mix well. Cook this barbecue sauce over low heat for 10
minutes.

Reduce heat to 325°.

Remove chicken from oven. Spread the chicken evenly with the
barbecue sauce. Return chicken to oven. Bake, uncovered, for
30 minutes.

Serves 4.

CHICKEN CHICAGO-STYLE

The following recipe is an adaptation of one we found in an old cookbook. There, it's described as "Fried Chicken." It's really an offhand version of a chicken saute, finished in the oven.

1 tablespoon salted butter
1 tablespoon bacon grease or
   lard
4 tablespoons all-purpose
   flour
$^1/_8$ teaspoon pepper
$^1/_4$ teaspoon salt
A $2^1/_2$ - to $3^1/_2$ - pound
   chicken, cut into serving
   pieces

Place the salted butter and bacon grease (or lard) in a heavy ovenproof skillet. Heat.

Mix the flour, pepper, and salt in a bag. Add the chicken and shake until evenly coated.

Preheat oven to 350°.

Lightly brown the chicken in the skillet, turning once or twice. Arrange the chicken so that it is skin-side-up in the skillet. Cover tightly and place in the oven. Cook for 45 minutes.

Serves 4.

CORNISH HENS

The brown rice stuffing provides a savory complement to the delicate flavor of the Cornish hens. If you prefer not to stuff the hens, season the cavity with freshly ground black pepper and lemon juice.

Two 1½-pound Cornish hens
Butter
Freshly ground black pepper
1 strip bacon

STUFFING
2 strips bacon
⅓ cup chopped onion
1 cup cooked brown rice
4 dates, pitted and chopped
2 tablespoons Madeira

For the stuffing, saute the bacon until not quite crisp. Add the onion and saute until it begins to lose its color. Add the bacon and onion to the rice. Add the dates and the Madeira. Mix well.

Stuff the hens loosely.

Preheat oven to 450°.

Truss the hens and rub well with butter. Season with pepper. Place one-half strip of bacon on the breast of each hen.

Place hens in oven. (First read **About Roasting and Broiling**.) Roast for 5 minutes.

Reduce heat to 325°. Roast for 50-60 minutes.

Serves 2.

ROAST TURKEY

You will have a difficult time finding a turkey as moist as that roasted in the convection oven. There is no need to use a self-basting turkey. Neither do you need to baste the turkey. Using the convection oven, lovers of dark meat may at last rediscover the taste of a juicy slice of white meat.

First, be sure the turkey will fit into your oven. If you have a large convection oven, you shouldn't have any problem. However, it is unlikely that you will be able to roast a turkey heavier than 13 pounds in the smaller convection ovens.

Roasting times for turkeys are, at best, approximate. What follows is, however, a fairly accurate schedule (for unstuffed turkeys).

WEIGHT IN POUNDS	ROASTING TIME
6-10	1½-2 hours
10-16	2-3¼ hours

For stuffed turkeys, add 3-5 minutes per pound to the roasting time.

Use a meat thermometer. An unstuffed turkey should be done when the temperature of the inner thigh reaches 180°-185°. Lacking a meat thermometer, you can test for doneness by pricking the thigh. If the juice runs clear, the turkey is done.

If the turkey has been stuffed, the internal temperature of the stuffing must reach 165°.

TO ROAST A TURKEY

Preheat oven to 450°.

Stuff the turkey, if it is to be stuffed.

Truss the turkey and rub it well with butter.

Place turkey in oven, breast side up. (First read **About Roasting and Broiling.**) Roast for 5 minutes.

Reduce heat to 300°.

Bake turkey according to the above schedule. Be sure to count into the roasting time the initial 5 minutes at 450°.

ROAST DUCK

A 4- to 6-pound duck
Salt
Freshly ground black pepper
2 stalks celery, chopped
6 juniper berries, crushed
1 clove garlic, halved
1 lemon, halved

Preheat oven to 450°.

Stuff the duck, if you desire.

If the duck is not to be stuffed, sprinkle the cavity with salt and pepper. Insert the celery and juniper berries.

Truss the duck, if necessary. You may need to tie only the wings.

Rub the duck well with the garlic and lemon. Season with pepper. Roast breast side up for 5 minutes. (First read **About Roasting and Broiling**.)

Reduce heat to 375°.

Roast about 15 minutes per pound for unstuffed duck. If duck is stuffed, add about 4 minutes per pound.

Serves 2 generously.

Vegetables

BROILED MUSHROOMS

Try to select mushrooms that are approximately the same size. This will ensure that they will all be finished at the same time. There is no need to trim the stems from the mushrooms. Broiled, they are as delicious as the caps. Before using, lightly wipe the mushrooms with a damp cloth.

20-30 medium mushrooms
  (cap diameter about 1½"-2")
3 tablespoons butter, melted
Salt
Freshly ground black pepper
Lemon juice

Preheat oven to 450°.

Coat the mushrooms well with the melted butter. Season with salt and pepper.

Broil for about 3-4 minutes. (First read **About Roasting and Broiling**.)

Sprinkle with lemon juice before serving, if desired.

Serves 4.

MUSHROOM AND BACON PIE

In this cookbook, we have tried to avoid recipes that require a considerable amount of preparation on top of the stove. This is one such dish. However, it is so good that we would have been negligent in leaving it out.

1 pie pastry
2 tablespoons butter
2$^1/_2$ cups chopped mushrooms
1 small onion, chopped fine
2 strips lean bacon
Salt
Freshly ground black pepper
3 eggs, separated
$^1/_4$ cup milk
$^1/_3$ cup grated Parmesan
    cheese

Preheat oven to 375°.

Line an 8″ pie plate with pie pastry. Prick well. Weight the pastry to prevent it from rising during baking.

Bake pastry about 20 minutes, or until lightly browned.

Boil the bacon for five minutes. Drain, and cut into small pieces about $^1/_4$″ square.

Melt the butter in a heavy skillet. Add the mushrooms and the onion. Saute until the mushrooms are heated through and the onions just begin to lose their color. Add the bacon and cook a few minutes longer. Season with salt and pepper to taste. Add the salt prudently, remembering that this dish includes bacon.

Beat the egg yolks slightly. Add the milk. Add this mixture to the mushrooms. Cook until mixture begins to thicken.

Pour mixture into the baked pie shell. Sprinkle with all but a few teaspoons of the Parmesan cheese.

Beat the egg whites until stiff, but not dry. Fold in the remaining Parmesan cheese.

Spread the beaten egg whites over the pie filling.

Bake at 375° for about 12 minutes. The top should be lightly browned.

Serves 4-6.

BAKED ZUCCHINI

2 large zucchini
1 tablespoon olive oil
Salt and pepper to taste
$^1/_4$ cup Swiss cheese, grated

Preheat oven to 300°.

Cut zucchini in half, lengthwise. Sprinkle with olive oil. Season with salt and pepper. Sprinkle with grated Swiss cheese. Place on a cookie sheet. Bake for 20 minutes.

Serves 4.

BROCCOLI CASSEROLE

This casserole is rich and very tasty. The bleu cheese adds zest, without dominating the flavor.

3 ounces cream cheese
3 ounces bleu cheese
2½ cups broccoli, chopped
   (or two 10-ounce packages
   frozen broccoli)
2 tablespoons butter
2 tablespoons all-purpose
   flour
⅔ cup milk
¼ teaspoon salt
⅛ teaspoon freshly ground
   black pepper

Preheat oven to 350°.

Cut the cream cheese and bleu cheese into small pieces.

Cook the broccoli in lightly salted water until tender. Drain.

Over low heat, melt the butter. Stir in the flour. Slowly add the milk, stirring steadily.

Gradually add the cream cheese and bleu cheese to the white sauce. Stir well to blend thoroughly. Season with the salt and pepper.

Place the broccoli in a small casserole (approximately 8″ x 8″ x 2″).

Pour the cheese sauce over the broccoli. Mix well.

Bake about 30 minutes.

Serves 6.

BROCCOLI SOUFFLE

3 eggs
2 tablespoons butter
2 tablespoons all-purpose
   flour
³/₄ cup milk
¹/₄ teaspoon freshly ground
   pepper
2 tablespoons onion, minced
1 cup mild cheese, minced
1 cup broccoli, cooked and
   chopped

Preheat oven to 350°.

Grease a 1-quart souffle dish. Separate the eggs and beat the yolks. Over low heat, melt the butter in a heavy saucepan. Stir in the flour. Add the milk a little at a time, stirring steadily to blend well. Add the pepper, onions, and cheese, stirring constantly until the cheese melts. Add the egg yolks and broccoli, stirring well. Cool slightly. Beat the egg whites with a whisk until stiff. Fold the egg whites carefully into the vegetable mixture. Pour into a 1-quart, greased souffle dish. Bake for 35 minutes.

Serves 4.

STUFFED GREEN PEPPERS OR TOMATOES

$^1/_2$ pound ground chuck
1 small onion, minced
$^1/_4$ cup cooked rice
$^1/_8$ teaspoon salt
$^1/_4$ teaspoon oregano
1 clove garlic, minced
4 medium green peppers or
    ripe tomatoes
2 ounces Monterey Jack or
    mozzarella cheese,
    chopped fine
1 teaspoon olive oil

Preheat oven to 375°.

Brown the ground chuck. Add the onion. Saute until it begins to lose its color. Add the rice, salt, oregano, and garlic.

If using green peppers, cut a circle around the stem end. Using a spoon, scoop out the seeds and membranes. If using tomatoes, do the same, being very careful not to puncture the skin.

Stuff the peppers (or tomatoes) by alternating layers of the beef-rice mixture with the cheese.

Lightly grease the bottom of a shallow baking dish with olive oil. Place the peppers or tomatoes in the baking dish. Bake peppers for 15 minutes. Bake tomatoes for 12 minutes.

Serves 4.

BAKED POTATOES
(SWEET AND OTHERWISE)

We have baked potatoes at various temperatures. They seem best when baked in a preheated oven at 375°. They are then cooked through, yet flaky and barely moist. At this temperature, a fairly large baking potato will be baked in about 45 minutes.

Before baking potatoes, wash them well. Dry them and grease them lightly. Pierce the skin in a few places.

OVEN-BROWNED POTATOES

These are vaguely similar to Potatoes Anna. However, they are not prepared in the classic pan. Neither are they turned. They are, nonetheless, simply excellent.

5 large potatoes, peeled
$^1/_4$ cup butter, melted
Salt
Freshly ground black pepper
Parmesan cheese, grated

Peel the potatoes and slice thin. Place in ice water for at least 20 minutes.

Preheat oven to 400°.

Butter a deep 9″ pie dish. Dry the potatoes. Arrange one layer, overlapping the potatoes. Sprinkle lightly with salt. Season with pepper. Sprinkle with Parmesan.

Arrange another layer of potatoes. Season with salt, pepper, and Parmesan cheese. Continue in this fashion until all potatoes are used.

Pour the melted butter over the potatoes. Bake, uncovered, for 25 minutes, or until top is deeply browned.

Serves 4.

JANSON'S TEMPTATION

2 tablespoons butter
5 medium potatoes, sliced
    into thin strips
2 medium onions, sliced thin
A 2-ounce can anchovy fillets
Freshly ground black pepper
1 cup light cream

Preheat oven to 350°.

Grease the pie dish with a little butter.

Place one-half of the potatoes in a 9″ pie dish. Spread them evenly, to cover the bottom. Cover the potatoes with the onions.

Drain the anchovy fillets, and reserve the juice. Chop them and spread them over the onions, distributing them evenly.

Cover the anchovies with the remaining potatoes. Season with the pepper. Dot with butter. Pour the reserved juice from the anchovies over the top.

Bake, uncovered, for 10 minutes.

Pour ½ cup cream over the potatoes.

Bake for another 10 minutes.

Pour the remaining cream over the potatoes. Bake, uncovered, for 25-30 minutes more.

Serves 4.

ACORN SQUASH

1 medium acorn squash
2 tablespoons butter
3 teaspoons brown sugar
¼ teaspoon salt

Preheat oven to 350°.

Cut the acorn squash in half. Scoop out the seeds. Place half of the butter, sugar, and salt in each squash half.

Place the squash in an ovenproof dish. Bake for 30 minutes.

Serves 2.

PEGGY'S GOLDMINES

A friend of ours introduced us to these in Brooklyn. She views them as a festive dish and serves them only on special occasions. We are not so discriminating.

4 slices white bread
4 thin slices of Swiss cheese
   (each slice approximately
   the same size as the bread
   slices)
4 large eggs

Preheat oven to 450°.

Place the slices of bread in a buttered baking dish. Cut a small circle (the size of an egg yolk) in the middle of each of the slices of Swiss cheese. Center a slice of cheese on each slice of bread.

Break one egg over each slice of bread. The yolk should be kept in place by the hole cut in the cheese.

Place the dish in the oven. Bake, uncovered, for five minutes or until the whites are firmly set. By this time, the cheese should have begun to melt. The yolks should have begun to set.

Serves 4.

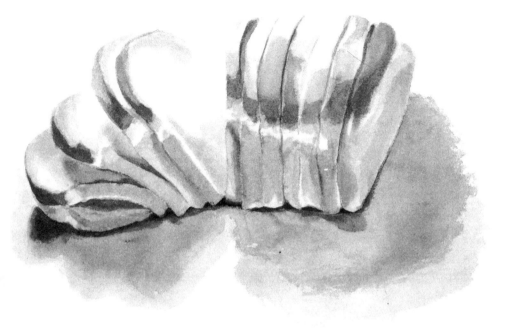

Bread

A WORD ON BREAD

The convection oven is particularly suited to the baking of breads. We feel no other oven can give such satisfying results. The circulating air bakes the bread evenly. You do not end up with bread that is done on the top, yet burned on the bottom.

All recipes given in CONVECTION OVEN COOKING use active dry yeast, usually sold in airtight foil packages. Some brands contain preservatives; others do not. As dry yeast will keep for a long time in a cool place, we have not seen the need to use those with preservatives. Each package contains approximately 1 tablespoon yeast. The water in which the yeast is dissolved should be warm (110°-115°), but not hot. Hot water will kill the yeast.

After the yeast is mixed with water, place it in a sheltered spot. It will bubble a little and eventually become foamy. At this point, it is ready to use.

Although it is not specifically mentioned in each recipe, we have used what is sometimes called the Cornell Formula. Developed by Dr. Clive McKay of Cornell, this formula makes bread more nutritious. For 16 percent of the flour called for in any given recipe, we have substituted:

8 percent powdered milk
6 percent soy flour
2 percent wheat germ

Roughly translated, this means that for every cup of flour, you would first place in the cup:

4 teaspoons powdered milk
1 tablespoon soy flour
1 teaspoon wheat germ

and fill the rest of the cup with flour.

If possible, use unbleached white flour. It is nutritionally preferable to the bleached white flour.

A WORD ON KNEADING

Kneading bread is one of the most rewarding aspects of baking. It is relaxing. With practice, you can learn a "feel" for the process and enjoy it even more.

There are as many different methods of kneading as there are breads. Every experienced baker has his or her personal method. There is, however, a simple way to begin. The dough should be kneaded firmly, but not roughly. The motion should be rhythmic and the kneading generally should take only about 8-10 minutes.

Dough is usually kneaded on a stable surface that has been dusted with flour. The most practical surface is a breadboard, although any smooth surface will do. Place the dough on the floured board and form it into a ball shape. Place the palm of your right hand (or left, if left-handed) in the lower center and push gently away from yourself, holding the dough in place with your free hand. The dough should resemble a misshapen catcher's mitt. Fold the dough back, turn it one-quarter turn and repeat the process.

The dough will be sticky at first, and you will need to keep your board well dusted with flour. Some recipes allot enough flour to be used for this purpose. However, conditions will vary, affecting the moisture content of your flour. Thus, flour quantities are always somewhat changeable, and you may need to add more while kneading. The general rule is to knead the dough until it no longer sticks to your fingers. A good dough that has been kneaded enough will be smooth and somewhat elastic. The more bread you make, the less you will need to consider when to stop. This is essentially all one needs to know.

When the dough is rising, it should be placed in a warm, draft-free spot. A draft can flatten any rising dough. It is important to keep the dough covered and away from any strong air currents. Covering the bowl with one or two clean towels is sufficient. A rack placed over the pilot light of a gas stove is an ideal spot to place your covered dough bowl.

In our recipes for yeast breads, we use the word *beat*. It is possible to mix and knead bread dough by using an electric mixer with a bread hook. However, in the later stages of the recipe, it may become difficult to continue without putting a strain on the machine. If this should happen, the recipe should be continued by hand. When used in yeast bread recipes in this cookbook, the word *beat* refers to the process of thoroughly stirring the flour into the batter, whether by hand or by machine.

Most of the bread recipes given here will freeze well for several weeks if double bagged. It is immensely helpful to slice the loaf *before* freezing, as the slices are then easily removed for the toaster.

For those who are making a yeast bread for the first time, **JACKIE'S EGG TWIST BREAD** is a good place to start.

WHITE BREAD

2 packages yeast
$^1/_3$ cup warm (not hot) water
1 cup milk
1 tablespoon butter, melted
2 tablespoons vegetable oil
1 tablespoon honey
2 teaspoons salt
1 cup orange juice
   (preferably freshly
   squeezed)
6-7 cups all-purpose flour

Dissolve the yeast in the warm water and set aside. Scald the milk and pour into a large bowl. Add the butter, vegetable oil, honey, and salt. Cool to lukewarm. When ready, add the yeast and the orange juice.

Add the flour gradually to the yeast mixture, beating until the dough begins to pull from the sides of the bowl (about 5 cups). Turn the dough out onto a board and knead in the remaining flour.

Place the dough in a greased bowl and turn so that it is greased on all sides. Cover and place in a warm spot to rise until doubled in size (about 1 hour).

Punch the dough down. Turn again, cover, and let rise for about 30 minutes or until doubled in size. Grease two $9^5/_8''$ x $5^1/_2''$ x $2^3/_4''$ loaf pans.

Turn out onto a lightly floured board, divide in half, and let rest for 10 minutes. Shape into loaves and place in the loaf pans. Allow to rise again for about 30 minutes, or until almost doubled in size.

Preheat oven to 350°.

Bake for 30 minutes. Remove from pans and set on racks to cool.

Makes 2 medium loaves.

JACKIE'S EGG TWIST BREAD

This bread has an impressive appearance. It will look like the work of a professional bakery—even on your first try. It is, however, one of the easiest yeast breads to make.

2 packages of yeast
$^1/_2$ cup warm water
1 tablespoon sugar
$^1/_2$ cup milk
2 tablespoons butter
1 tablespoon sugar
2 teaspoons salt
3 eggs, slightly beaten
$4^1/_2$-5 cups all-purpose flour
1 egg white

Dissolve the yeast in $^1/_2$ cup warm water and 1 tablespoon sugar.

Scald the milk and add the butter and 1 tablespoon sugar. Pour into a mixing bowl and allow to cool to lukewarm. Stir in the yeast mixture. Add the salt, then the 3 slightly beaten eggs. Stir in the flour gradually until mixture begins to pull away from sides of bowl (about 4 cups). Turn the dough onto a well-floured board and knead in the remaining flour. Knead until the dough is smooth and no longer sticky.

Place the dough into a greased bowl and turn so that all sides are greased. Cover, and place in a warm spot to rise for 1 hour, or until nearly doubled.

Punch down, and divide in half (for 2 loaves). Let rest for 10 minutes. Divide each half into three parts and form into lengths.

Braid dough. To braid, start from the middle and work out to one end, then the other. Pinch together the three lengths at both ends. Place on a greased cookie sheet. Cover, and let rise until doubled in size.

Preheat oven to 325°.

Brush the loaves with the white of 1 egg and bake for 30 minutes. (Bake for 35 minutes if making 1 large loaf.)

Makes 2 medium loaves or 1 large loaf.

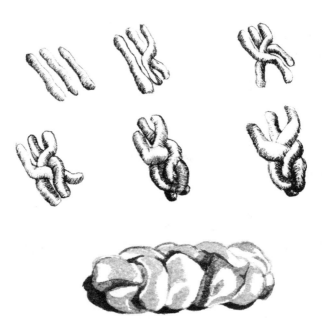

OATMEAL BREAD

This bread is somewhat heavier than others in this cookbook. It slices well and is good for toasting.

2 packages yeast
$^1/_2$ cup warm (not hot) water
$2^1/_2$ cups milk
$^1/_4$ cup sugar
$^1/_4$ cup butter
2 teaspoons salt
$2^1/_2$ cups rolled oats
3-4 cups graham flour
2 cups all-purpose white flour

Mix the yeast in the warm water and set to rise. Scald the milk and pour into a large bowl. Add the sugar, butter, and salt. Cool to lukewarm. Measure the rolled oats, graham flour, and white flour. Mix.

Pour the yeast mixture into the cooled milk, sugar, butter, and salt. Stir in the flours and the rolled oats a cup at a time. Turn the dough out onto a floured board and knead well. Use more flour, if necessary. Place dough in a greased bowl. Turn dough to grease all sides. Cover, and set to rise. Grease two $9^5/_8$" x $5^1/_2$" x $2^3/_4$" loaf pans.

When doubled in size (about 1 hour), punch down the dough and cut in half. Form into loaves and place into the loaf pans. Cover and allow to double in size (about 30 minutes).

Preheat oven to 300°.

Brush with a little melted butter and bake for 55 minutes.

Makes 2 medium loaves.

CINNAMON-RAISIN BREAD

This makes a large loaf that slices and freezes well. It is delicious toasted and buttered. Recipe may be doubled—but a very large bowl must be used and 5-10 minutes added to the baking time.

1 package yeast
$^1/_4$ cup warm (not hot) water
$3^1/_2$ cups all-purpose flour
1 teaspoon salt
$1^1/_2$ cups raisins
$^3/_4$ cup milk, scalded
$^1/_3$ cup butter (about $5^1/_2$
   tablespoons)
$^1/_4$ cup honey
1 egg
FILLING:
2 tablespoons melted butter
3 tablespoons maple syrup
2 teaspoons cinnamon
$^1/_4$ teaspoon nutmeg
$^1/_8$ teaspoon allspice

Dissolve the yeast in warm water. Sift flour and salt together. Wash, drain, and dry the raisins.

Scald the milk and stir in the butter and honey. Pour into a large bowl and cool to lukewarm. Stir in a slightly beaten egg, then the yeast mixture. Add $^1/_2$ of the sifted flour and salt, mixing thoroughly. Cover and let sit in a warm place for $1^1/_2$ hours, or until light and spongy.

Mix the drained raisins with the remaining flour.

When the dough is light, and bubbles begin to form on top, stir down. Beat in as much as possible of the remaining flour and raisin mixture. Turn onto a floured board and knead in the remainder until dough is elastic and raisins well distributed. If dough is sticky, use more flour.

Put into a large greased bowl, turn dough over once so that all sides are greased. Cover, and put in a warm spot for a second rising (about $1^{1}/_{2}$ hours, or until nearly doubled).

Grease a $9^{5}/_{8}''$ x $5^{1}/_{2}''$ x $2^{3}/_{4}''$ loaf pan and set aside. In a small saucepan, melt the butter and add the maple syrup and the spice mixture. Cool.

When ready, punch the dough down, and roll into a rectangular shape roughly the width of your bread pan. Brush syrup mixture well over surface of dough, although not to the edges. Roll tightly, pinching the ends well together. Don't worry if some of the mixture escapes, although you must work quickly. Be sure the pinched side is on the bottom of the pan and both pinched ends are tucked well under.

Place in the greased loaf pan. Brush the top with any remaining filling. Cover and set to rise until almost doubled.

Preheat oven to 300°

When ready, bake for 50-60 minutes. Remove from pan and cool.

Makes 1 large loaf.

CRACKED WHOLE-WHEAT BREAD

This bread is delicious and freezes well.

$^1/_2$ cup cracked whole wheat
$1^1/_2$ cups water
1 package yeast
$^1/_2$ cup warm (not hot) water
1 teaspoon sugar
4 cups all-purpose white flour
3 cups whole-wheat flour
$^3/_4$ cup cornmeal
$^1/_2$ cup powdered milk
2 teaspoons salt
1 egg
$^1/_4$ cup butter
$^1/_4$ cup molasses
$1^1/_2$ cups hot water
Butter

Put the cracked wheat and $1^1/_2$ cups water into a saucepan. Boil for about 20 minutes, stirring occasionally. When tender, raise the heat and boil until all water is absorbed, stirring vigorously. Combine the yeast, $^1/_2$ cup warm water, and 1 teaspoon sugar and put aside. In a large bowl, mix the white flour and whole-wheat flour. Add the cornmeal, powdered milk, and salt. Stir until thoroughly mixed.

Into a large bowl, put 1 slightly beaten egg, $^1/_4$ cup butter, $^1/_4$ cup molasses, and $1^1/_2$ cups very hot water. Stir until all is dissolved. Into this put the cooked cracked wheat. Stir and cool to lukewarm. Pour in the yeast mixture. Add the flour, cornmeal, powdered milk, and salt mixture to the above, a cup at a time, stirring until too stiff to continue. If any flour remains, knead it in. Turn dough out onto a well-floured board and knead until it is elastic and no longer sticky.

Grease a large bowl and put in the dough. Turn the dough over, so that it becomes greased on the top. Cover well and set in a warm place to rise. After the dough has almost doubled in size (about 30 minutes), turn out and lightly knead down. Divide in half and let rest for 10 minutes. Grease two $9^5/_8''$ x $5^1/_2''$ x $2^3/_4''$ loaf pans.

Form into 2 loaves and place in the loaf pans. Let rise until almost doubled in size (about 30 minutes). Brush with melted butter just before baking.

Preheat oven to 275°.

Bake for 1 hour. When done, turn out of pans onto racks to cool. Be sure loaves are thoroughly cooled before freezing.

Makes 2 medium loaves.

CORNBREAD

1 cup milk
2 tablespoons honey (may be
    omitted if you prefer
    unsweetened cornbread)
2 tablespoons vegetable oil
$^3/_4$ cup all-purpose flour,
    sifted
2 teaspoons baking powder
$^1/_2$ teaspoon salt
$1^1/_4$ cups white or yellow
    stone-ground cornmeal
2 eggs
$1^1/_2$ cups whole-kernel corn
    (17-ounce can), drained

Preheat oven to 350°.

Grease a 10″ heavy round iron skillet (3″ deep) and place in the heated oven. Warm the milk slightly and add the honey and oil. Into a medium bowl, resift the flour with the baking powder and salt. Add the cornmeal. Beat the 2 eggs slightly and add to the milk mixture. Add this all at once to the dry ingredients. Stir well and add the drained corn. Remove the skillet from the oven. Pour in the batter. Bake for 25 minutes.

Leftover cornbread? Try the following recipe.

2 cups milk, scalded
$^1/_2$ tablespoon butter
1 tablespoon honey
   (optional)
1 cup cornbread crumbs
2 eggs, beaten
A few dashes of salt

Preheat oven to 325°.

Melt the butter in the scalded milk. Stir in the honey. Pour this mixture over the bread crumbs. Add the eggs and salt. Stir well and pour into a greased pan. Bake for 35 minutes.

RAISIN QUICK BREAD (IRISH)

If you have unexpected guests for breakfast, this is the bread to serve. It is simple to prepare, and you can be assured that none will be left. Recipe may be doubled.

2 cups all-pupose flour, sifted
3 teaspoons baking powder
$^1/_2$ teaspoon salt
$^1/_4$ cup sugar
$^1/_4$ cup butter
$^1/_2$ cup raisins or chopped
    dates
1 egg, slightly beaten
$^2/_3$ cup milk

Preheat oven to 325°.

Grease one cookie sheet. Sift all dry ingredients into a large bowl. Cut in the butter until well blended. Stir in the raisins. Beat the egg and milk together, and stir into the dry mixture. Turn out all at once onto the cookie sheet and place immediately into the preheated oven. The dough should not be spread onto the cookie sheet. Rather, its form should be kept as compact as possible. Bake for 30-40 minutes.

Makes 1 round loaf.

FLORENCE'S SOUR CREAM COFFEE CAKE

This makes a nice, rich coffee cake, suitable for any occasion.

1 cup butter
1 cup sugar
2 eggs
1 teaspoon vanilla
2 cups all-purpose flour,
    sifted
1 teaspoon baking powder
1 teaspoon baking soda
$\frac{1}{2}$ teaspoon salt
1 cup sour cream
$\frac{1}{4}$ cup sugar
1 teaspoon cinnamon
$\frac{1}{3}$ cup brown sugar
1 cup broken pecan meats

Cream the butter and 1 cup of sugar in a large bowl until light. Add the eggs one at a time and beat. Add the vanilla. Resift the flour with the baking powder, baking soda, and salt. Alternate adding this with the sour cream to the butter and sugar mixture.

Preheat oven to 300°.

Mix $\frac{1}{4}$ cup white sugar, cinnamon, brown sugar, and pecan meats. Grease a 9" x 13" dish and lightly dust with flour. Pour in half of the batter. Sprinkle with half of the cinnamon mixture. Add the remaining batter and top with the rest of the cinnamon mixture. Bake for 35-40 minutes.

Makes one 9" x 13" cake.

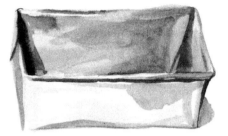

VERY MOIST APPLESAUCE BREAD

$^1/_2$ cup butter
1 cup sugar
1 egg
2 cups cake flour, sifted
1 teaspoon baking soda
$^1/_2$ teaspoon salt
$^1/_2$ teaspoon cinnamon
$^1/_4$ teaspoon cloves
$1^1/_2$ cups applesauce
1 teaspoon vanilla
1 cup dates, finely sliced
1 cup chopped nuts
1 cup raisins

Preheat oven to 300°.

Grease a $9^5/_8''$ x $5^1/_2''$ x $2^3/_4''$ loaf pan. Cream the butter and sugar in a large bowl. Add the egg and beat thoroughly. Sift the flour once, and resift with the baking soda, salt, and spices. Alternate adding the flour mixture and the applesauce to the butter, sugar, and egg mixture. After each addition, beat until smooth. Add the vanilla, dates, nuts, and raisins. Pour into the loaf pan and bake for 1 hour and 20 minutes.

Makes 1 large loaf.

Rolls, Muffins, and Biscuits

SWEET BUNS

These buns have a delicate honey flavor, but are not too sweet to be used as dinner rolls. If sugar is preferred, substitute $\frac{1}{3}$ cup sugar for the 4 tablespoons of honey.

1 package yeast
$\frac{1}{4}$ cup warm (not hot) water
1 tablespoon sugar
1 cup milk, scalded
$4\frac{1}{2}$ cups all-purpose flour,
    sifted
4 tablespoons honey
3 tablespoons butter
$\frac{1}{2}$ teaspoon lemon juice
1 egg, slightly beaten
1 teaspoon salt

Dissolve the yeast, warm water, and sugar. Set aside to rise. Scald the milk and pour into a large bowl. Cool to lukewarm. Add the yeast mixture. Resift the flour and add about 2 cups of flour. Stir in well. Cover and set in a warm place to rise.

When the sponge is light and bubbles start to form on the top (about 45 minutes), stir down. Add the honey, lemon juice, and the slightly beaten egg. Stir in well. Sift the salt with the remaining flour and add to the dough. Turn out onto a floured board and knead well.

Cover and let rise until doubled in size (about 45 minutes). Punch down and shape into rolls. Let rise once more until almost doubled (about 30 minutes).

Preheat oven to 300°.

Bake for about 18 minutes.

Makes 18 large buns.

HOT CROSS BUNS FOR KEVIN

For a different taste, try adding nutmeg or raisins to the dough before the last rising. Recipe may be doubled or tripled.

1 package yeast
$\frac{1}{4}$ cup warm (not hot) water
1 cup milk, scalded
$\frac{1}{2}$ teaspoon honey (or 1
   teaspoon sugar)
$\frac{1}{4}$ teaspoon salt
3-4 cups all-purpose flour
3 tablespoons butter
$2\frac{1}{2}$ tablespoons honey (or $\frac{1}{3}$
   cup sugar)
1 egg white
3-5 teaspoons sugar

Dissolve the yeast in the $\frac{1}{4}$ cup of warm water and set aside. Scald the milk. Pour into a large bowl and add the $\frac{1}{2}$ teaspoon honey (or 1 teaspoon sugar) and salt. Cool to lukewarm. Stir in the yeast. Add enough flour to make a light batter (about $1\frac{1}{2}$ - 2 cups flour). Cover and allow to rise (about 30 minutes).

Melt 3 tablespoons butter and add $2\frac{1}{2}$ tablespoons honey (or $\frac{1}{3}$ cup sugar). After the batter has risen, work it up lightly and stir in the melted butter mixture. Add the remaining flour. Turn out onto a floured board and knead thoroughly. Cover and set to rise until light, or almost doubled in size (20-30 minutes).

Punch down, and roll out to about $\frac{1}{2}''$ thick and cut with a 3'' biscuit cutter. Place on a greased cookie sheet to rise until light (about 5-10 minutes).

Preheat oven to 350°.

With a sharp knife, cut a cross on the top of each bun. Bake approximately 10 minutes. Take out the buns and brush the tops with 1 egg white mixed with sugar (3-5 teaspoons). Return to the oven and bake 5 minutes longer.

Makes about 15 buns.

REFRIGERATOR ROLLS

These rolls are easy to make. The dough will last several days in the refrigerator.

1 cup boiling water
$\frac{1}{8}$ cup sugar or 3 tablespoons
    honey
3 tablespoons butter
$\frac{1}{2}$ tablespoon salt
1 package yeast
$\frac{1}{2}$ teaspoon sugar
$\frac{1}{4}$ cup warm (not hot) water
1 egg, slightly beaten
4 cups all-purpose flour,
    sifted

Boil the water and pour into a large bowl. Mix in the sugar (or honey), butter, and salt. Cool until lukewarm. Dissolve the package of yeast and $1/2$ teaspoon sugar in $1/4$ cup warm water and set to rise. When ready, add to the first mixture. Add the slightly beaten egg.

Resift the flour and add. Stir in thoroughly, but do not knead. Grease another bowl and place dough in it. Cover and place in refrigerator.

When ready to use, shape into rolls and place on a greased pan. Let rise for about $1/2$ hour, or until doubled in size.

Preheat oven to 350°.

Bake for 15-20 minutes.

Makes about 2 dozen rolls.

PARKER HOUSE ROLLS

Soft rolls, these have a nice texture and a delicate egg flavor. They are excellent as dinner rolls.

1 package yeast
$1/2$ cup warm water
$1/2$ cup milk
2 tablespoons butter
2 tablespoons sugar (or 1
    tablespoon honey)
$1^1/2$ teaspoons salt
2 egg yolks
4 cups all-purpose flour
$1^1/2$ tablespoons melted
    butter

Dissolve the yeast in the warm water and set aside.

Scald the milk. Pour into a mixing bowl and add the butter, sugar (or honey), and salt. Cool to lukewarm.

Add the yeast. Beat the egg yolks slightly and add. Stir in the flour. Turn out onto a floured board and knead until smooth and no longer sticky. Add more flour if necessary.

Place the dough in a greased bowl. To prevent a crust from forming, turn dough to grease entire surface. Cover, and let rise until doubled in size (about 1½ hours). When dough has doubled in size, punch down, work lightly, and allow to rest for 5 minutes.

Roll to ⅓″ thickness. Cut with a medium-sized (2″) biscuit cutter. Place on a greased cookie sheet.

With the back of a spoon, lightly press the middle of each circle of dough. Brush with the melted butter. Fold each circle almost in half, so that the top edge rests just inside the bottom edge. Seal gently with the tips of your fingers. Brush the tops with any butter that remains. Cover, and allow to rise for 45 minutes or until doubled in size.

Preheat oven to 350°.

Bake for 15 minutes.

Makes approximately 35 medium-sized rolls.

CRUSTY ROLLS

These rolls are very chewy.

1 package yeast
$^1/_4$ cup warm (not hot) water
$^3/_4$ cup boiling water
1 tablespoon sugar
$1^1/_2$ teaspoons salt
2 tablespoons butter
$3^1/_2$ cups all-purpose flour
2 eggs
White cornmeal
1 tablespoon water

Dissolve the yeast in the warm water. Pour the boiling water into a bowl and stir in the sugar, salt, and butter until dissolved. Cool to lukewarm. Add the yeast. Beat in 1 cup of flour.

Separate the eggs. Beat the egg whites with a whisk until stiff. Fold into the yeast mixture. Beat in the remaining $2^1/_2$ cups of flour. Turn dough out onto a floured board and knead until dough is no longer sticky. Add more flour, if necessary. Dough should be smooth and satiny.

Place dough in a greased bowl. Turn dough so that all sides are greased. Cover well. Place in a warm, draft-free spot to rise until almost doubled in size (about 45 minutes).

Punch down and let rest 10 minutes. Sprinkle a cookie sheet with the cornmeal. Divide the dough into 24 pieces and roll into balls. Place on the cookie sheet. Cover and allow to rise until nearly doubled in size (about 30 minutes).

Preheat oven to 425°.

Beat the egg yolks slightly and add 1 tablespoon water. Brush the rolls with this mixture just before baking. Bake for 15 minutes. Reduce heat to 350°. Bake for 5 minutes.

Makes 24 rolls.

BREAD CRUMB MUFFINS

$1/4$ cup ripe banana, mashed
$2/3$ cup milk
1 cup dry bread crumbs
$1/3$ cup raisins
$1/2$ cup all-purpose flour, sifted
2 teaspoons baking powder
$1/2$ teaspoon salt
$1/2$ tablespoon butter
1 egg
2 tablespoons sugar

Preheat oven to 350°.

Grease the muffin tins. Mash the banana and mix with the milk. Pour this over the bread crumbs and the raisins. Let soak for 10 minutes. Into a medium bowl, resift the flour with the baking powder and salt.

Melt the butter and lightly beat in the egg and sugar. Add the bread crumb mixture. Add this all at once to the dry ingredients and mix only until all is moistened. Partly fill tins and bake for 15 minutes.

Makes 1 dozen muffins.

LEMON-SWEET MUFFINS

For those who find only the sweetest to be best.

1 cup butter
²/₃ cup sugar
4 eggs
¹/₂ teaspoon vanilla
¹/₄ cup lemon juice
2 cups all-purpose flour,
    sifted
2 teaspoons baking powder
1 teaspoon salt
2 teaspoons grated lemon
    peel
Sugar

Lightly grease the muffin tins. Cream the butter and sugar. Separate the eggs and reserve the whites. Beat the egg yolks well and add to the butter-sugar mixture. Add the vanilla. Beat until light.

Squeeze the whole lemon and measure. Save the grated peel for the egg whites. Resift the flour with the baking powder and salt. Alternate adding the flour mixture and the lemon juice to the butter, sugar, and egg mixture. Mix well.

Preheat oven to 300°.

Beat the egg whites and lemon peel until stiff. Fold in. Fill the lightly greased muffin tins about three-quarters full. Sprinkle the tops with sugar. Bake for 20-25 minutes.

Makes about 18 large muffins.

MUFFIN SURPRISE

Experiment! Try with chopped dates, nuts, dried fruit, or raisins.

2 cups all-purpose flour,
   sifted
$^1/_2$ teaspoon salt
$2^1/_2$ teaspoons baking powder
1 egg
2 tablespoons honey
4 tablespoons shortening
   (butter or oil)
1 cup milk

Preheat oven to 350°.

Grease the muffin tins. Into a medium-sized bowl, resift the flour with the salt and baking powder. Beat the egg slightly and add the honey, melted shortening, and milk. Pour this mixture all at once into the dry ingredients. Stir only until all is moistened. Pour into tins and bake for 25 minutes.

Makes 1 dozen muffins.

"FAMILY-STYLE" MUFFIN AND BISCUIT MIX

If your family likes hot biscuits or muffins on a regular basis, it is wise to be prepared by premixing a large batch to keep on hand.

9 cups all-purpose flour,
   sifted
1/3 cup baking powder
   (double acting)
1 tablespoon salt
1/4 cup sugar
1 teaspoon cream of tartar
1 3/4 cups shortening that
   does not need refrigeration

Sift all of the dry ingredients together 3 or 4 times. Cut in the shortening until the mixture has reached the consistency of cornmeal. Store in a tightly covered container. Makes 13 cups.

MUFFINS FROM MIX

3 cups "FAMILY-STYLE"
   MUFFIN AND BISCUIT
   MIX
2 tablespoons sugar
1 egg
1 cup milk

Preheat oven to 350°.

Grease the muffin tins. Add the sugar to the mix and place in a medium bowl. Beat the egg slightly and add to the milk. Pour this all at once into the dry ingredients and mix until all is moistened. Spoon into greased muffin tins and bake for 20 minutes.

Makes 1 dozen muffins.

BISCUITS FROM MIX

1½ cups **"FAMILY-STYLE" MUFFIN AND BISCUIT MIX**
⅓ cup milk

Preheat oven to 375°.

Add the milk to the mix and stir well. Turn onto a floured board and knead lightly. Fold dough and roll to about ½″ thick. Cut with a biscuit cutter. Bake on a cookie sheet for 10 minutes.

Makes 10 biscuits.

CREAM BISCUITS

Light and flaky, these biscuits have never failed.

2 cups all-purpose flour, sifted
½ teaspoon salt
2½ teaspoons baking powder
1 tablespoon butter
¾ cup cream

Preheat oven to 375°.

Resift the flour, adding the salt and baking powder. Rub in the butter with the tips of your fingers. Make a "well" in the center and pour in the cream. Stir quickly until all is absorbed. Turn out onto a floured board. Knead lightly. Roll out or pat out to a thickness of about ½″. Fold, and roll again. Cut with a 3″ biscuit cutter. Bake on a cookie sheet for 10-12 minutes.

Makes 1 dozen biscuits.

DROP BISCUITS

For these biscuits, no kneading or rolling is needed. They are light in both taste and texture.

1½ cups all-purpose flour,
    sifted
1¾ teaspoons baking powder
¼ teaspoon salt
1 tablespoon butter
¾ cup milk

Preheat oven to 375°.

Grease a baking sheet. Resift the flour, adding the baking powder and salt. Rub the butter into the flour mixture with the tips of your fingers. Pour in the milk all at once, and stir well. Drop the dough from a tablespoon onto the greased baking sheet. Biscuits should be about an inch apart. Bake for 12-15 minutes.

Makes approximately 1 dozen biscuits.

SOUR CREAM BISCUITS

This is an especially light dough. It must be handled gently and quickly.

2 cups all-purpose flour,
   sifted
1 teaspoon baking soda
$1/4$ teaspoon salt
$1/2$ cup sour cream
$1/2$ cup buttermilk

Preheat oven to 375°.

Resift the flour, adding the baking soda and the salt. With a knife, loosely cut in the sour cream until well distributed. Pour in the buttermilk and stir quickly.

Turn out onto a floured board and knead very lightly, barely pressing on the dough. Roll out to thickness of $1/2''$. Fold, and roll once more. Cut with a 3″ biscuit cutter. Place on a cookie sheet and bake 10-12 minutes.

Makes 1 dozen biscuits.

Pastries, Pies, and One Custard

PUFF PASTRY

Most recipes for puff pastry instill such fear at the outset that one is hesitant even to begin. There is no reason to be intimidated, however. Making puff pastry is a simple process. To avoid confusion, these directions are more lengthy than most. Follow them carefully and you should have perfect and delicious results.

Puff pastry is most successfully made under the coldest possible conditions. Generally speaking, it is not a summertime project. To achieve best results, all utensils should be refrigerated. A marble slab is the ideal working surface. Whatever is used, however, should be kept as cold as possible.

PUFF PASTRY

2 cups all-purpose flour,
    sifted
$1/4$ teaspoon salt
$1/2$ cup unsalted butter (no
    substitutes)
$2/3$ cup ice water

Resift the flour with the salt into a large bowl. Cover and refrigerate. Refrigerate the rolling pin. Have ready a piece of wax paper.

Put the butter into a bowl of cold water. Squeeze the butter until soft, shaking off all excess water. Shape into a block about 4″ x 6″. Dust lightly with flour. Wrap in the wax paper and refrigerate.

Remove the bowl of flour and salt from the refrigerator. Gradually add the ice water, mixing it in with a knife until all is thoroughly mixed. Lightly form into a ball and refrigerate for 20 minutes. Before the next step, it is important to note that the butter and the dough must have the same consistency before being worked. The butter should be as soft and pliable as the dough. Both should be well chilled.

Remove the dough, butter, and rolling pin from the refrigerator. If the butter has become too hard, knead it a little in the wax paper so that it has the same consistency as the dough.

Roll the dough into a rectangular shape, roughly 6″ x 16″. It is a good idea to use a ruler at first, as it helps to avoid complications later.

Unwrap and place the brick of butter crosswise in the middle of the rectangle of dough. Fold one end of the dough over the butter and seal (crimp) the edges. Do the same for the other end. The butter should be well sealed, envelope-style, within the rectangle. Wrap in wax paper and refrigerate for 20 minutes.

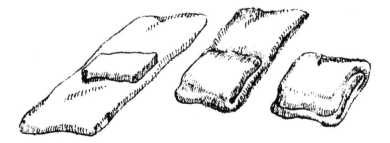

Flour your working surface, using as little flour as possible. This will help prevent sticking. Remove the dough and enclosed butter and place a narrow, crimped edge closest to you. Roll out to a 6" x 16" rectangle. When rolling, start with short, light strokes, keeping the motion constant and avoiding uneven pressure. Be careful not to let one hand press more heavily than the other. Roll quickly, but don't roll completely to the ends.

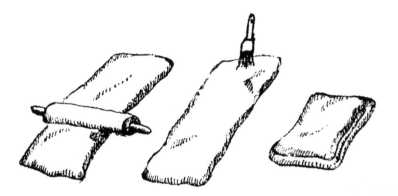

The butter should start to show through by the time you have rolled out this rectangle. It is very important that the butter never breaks through while rolling. Puff pastry depends on trapped moisture to create steam. This, in turn, raises the various layers. Letting the butter break through while rolling breaks this seal, and the pastry will not rise. This is the main reason for keeping everything as cold as possible.

If the butter should break through, flour the spot heavily and roll it in with the rolling pin. You may patch with a piece of dough taken from the end. However, we find the flour to be more effective.

After rolling the dough into a rectangular shape, brush off all excess flour. A pastry brush is excellent for this. Fold the dough into thirds (letter-style). Wrap in wax paper and refrigerate for 30 minutes.

Take out the dough. Place folded edges to either side. Open edges should be facing you. The dough is now one-quarter turn from where it was the last time you worked on it. Roll out in the same manner as before. Brush and fold. Refrigerate for 30 minutes.

Repeat this process (roll, fold, refrigerate) three more times. Mark each of these operations on a piece of paper so that you do not lose count.

The dough may now be frozen for 3-4 months or refrigerated for 2-3 days. It is best to refrigerate it for several hours (preferably overnight) before using.

This is all there is to puff pastry. If you have enjoyed making and eating your pastries, you might become very practiced in the art of pastry making. There are a few short cuts that may be used after you have become accustomed to the process. It is possible (under very cold conditions!) to make two rolls, or "turns", in one operation, without a 30-minute wait in between. However, you must work quickly so that your dough does not warm up and allow the butter to break through. Also, the freezer may be used instead of the refrigerator to cool the dough between turns. However, the dough must be checked to ensure that it does not become too hard.

note:

Before each of the following recipes, roll out the dough one more time before baking. When cutting the dough, the knife or pizza cutter must be thin, hot, and *very sharp*. The slightest drag in cutting will keep the pastry from rising at that edge.

PASTRY FILLING

2 cups milk
5 egg yolks
5 ounces sugar
$\frac{1}{2}$ cup all-purpose flour,
    sifted
$\frac{1}{2}$ teaspoon salt
1 teaspoon vanilla (or 2
    tablespoons rum, kirsch,
    or brandy)

Scald the milk and cool. Beat the egg yolks and sugar until they are light yellow in color. Resift the flour with the salt, and add. Slowly pour the milk into the mixture of yolks, sugar, flour, and salt. When all are combined, pour the mixture back into the saucepan and cook over low heat until thickened. When cool, add the flavoring.

PUFF PASTRY TWISTS

Whenever you trim your pastry to size before baking, save the ends. They are delicious when given a twist, placed on the baking sheet, and sprinkled with cinnamon and sugar. Bake as you would any puff pastry.

NAPOLEONS

Roll out 1 **PUFF PASTRY** to ¹/₈″ thick and about 18″ long. Using a hot pizza cutter, or a thin, very sharp knife, trim all edges to make a rectangle.

Divide the rectangle into four strips about 2¹/₂″ wide and 18″ long. Divide in half, crosswise. You now have 8 strips, each approximately 2¹/₂″ wide and 9″ long.

Refrigerate all the slices for 30 minutes. The size of your oven will dictate the number of strips you can bake at one time. It is important not to restrict the air flow. This gives the pastry the best chance of rising. We often bake only a few strips at a time for this reason. A rimless cookie sheet is good to bake on.

The oven must be very hot. Preheat to 450°.

Reduce heat to 425° just before baking. Bake for 10-15 minutes. Watch your pastries carefully. This is a needless instruction. You probably won't be able to take your eyes off them. They are so much fun to watch rise. Take care that they do not burn. (They burn quite easily.) They should be lightly browned and fluffy when finished. Cool on a rack.

When cool, cut crosswise to whatever length you desire. Cover one-half with **PASTRY FILLING** and top with the remaining pieces.

If you wish, the tops may be covered with a frosting of:

1 cup confectioner's sugar,
    sifted
¹/₂ teaspoon vanilla
1¹/₂ tablespoons boiling water

Mix. Spoon over the tops and refrigerate.

When frosting has cooled, dribble the following mixture over the frosting, forming a checkerboard pattern. Take the following:

1 square chocolate
1 teaspoon butter
1 tablespoon water

Melt all of the above in a double boiler. Remove Napoleons from refrigerator and dribble the chocolate mixture over the white frosting, forming a checkerboard pattern.

APPLE TURNOVERS

1 PUFF PASTRY
3-4 apples, peeled and sliced
$^1/_2$ cup sugar
1 tablespoon cornstarch
1 teaspoon lemon juice
$^1/_4$ teaspoon cinnamon
$^1/_4$ teaspoon cloves
1 egg
1 tablespoon water

Mix the apples, sugar, cornstarch, lemon juice, and spices in a saucepan. Cook over low heat until the apples are tender. Chill in the refrigerator.

Roll the puff pastry to about $1/8''$ thick, rolling evenly. Trim edges with a pizza cutter or a thin, very sharp knife to form a rectangle. Divide into six sections 6" square. Brush with a mixture of egg and 1 tablespoon water. Be careful not to brush over the edges, however.

Spoon out the chilled apple mixture into the center of the squares (not going near the edges) and fold in half. Or, if you desire, fold in half diagonally so that they form a triangle. Seal the edges well. The edges must be tightly crimped. Place in the refrigerator for 30 minutes or in the freezer for 15-20 minutes.

Preheat oven to 450°.

Bake for 10 minutes. Reduce heat to 350° and bake 5 minutes more.

Makes 6 turnovers.

A SPECIAL BIRTHDAY CAKE

Roll out one **PUFF PASTRY** into a rectangle $1/8''$ thick. Take a 9" cake pan. Place this on top of the puff pastry. Cut around the pan with a pizza cutter or a thin, very sharp knife. There should be enough pastry for two 9" circles. Prick well with a fork and refrigerate for 30 minutes.

Preheat oven to 450°.

Reduce heat to 425°. Bake for 15-20 minutes, watching carefully.

Makes two 9" round layers.

FILLING
2 cups fresh strawberries,
   halved lengthwise
$^1/_2$ **PASTRY FILLING** with
   1 tablespoon brandy

Drain the strawberries if frozen. Spread pastry filling on one of the 9″ circles and arrange the strawberries, reserving the best berries for the top. Cover with the remaining circle and arrange the better strawberries in the center.

If a richer cake is desired, make the whole recipe of **PASTRY FILLING** with 2 tablespoons brandy. Slit the circles, making 4 circles. Fill each layer with filling and strawberries. Decorate the top as shown for **NAPOLEONS.**

PIE PASTRY I

This recipe makes a 9″ double-crust. Divide it in half for a single crust.

2 cups all-purpose flour,
   sifted
$^1/_2$ teaspoon salt
$^1/_4$ cup solid shortening or
   lard
$^1/_2$ cup butter
4-5 tablespoons water

Resift the flour, adding the salt. Cut in the shortening or lard and the butter until the mixture has reached the consistency of cornmeal.

Gradually add the water, stirring with a knife. Lightly form into a ball. Turn out onto a well-floured board and roll.

PIE PASTRY II

This recipe will make one 8″ crust.

1 cup all-purpose flour, sifted
$^1/_2$ teaspoon salt
$^1/_3$ cup solid shortening or
   lard
3-4 tablespoons cold water

Resift the flour, adding the salt. Cut in the shortening or lard and the butter until the mixture has the consistency of cornmeal.

Gradually add the water, stirring with a knife. Lightly form into a ball. Turn out onto a well-floured board and roll.

PIE PASTRY III

This pie pastry is a gem. It is easy to make and very flaky. This recipe will make three 9″ crusts, and one lattice—depending on the depth of your pie dish.

3 cups all-purpose flour,
   sifted
$^1/_2$ cup butter
$^1/_2$ cup solid shortening or
   lard
$^3/_4$ cup ice water

Resift the flour into a bowl. Cut in the butter and shortening.

Sprinkle in all of the water, turning the dough constantly with a knife. Turn dough out onto a well-floured board. Pat it very gently until it holds together. Lightly dust the top with flour. Roll out the dough to a thickness of $1/2''$. Fold one end toward the middle. Then fold the other. Use a knife if the dough sticks. The dough should now be folded into thirds, envelope-style. Using the knife, lift the dough from the board. Dust the board again with flour. Replace the dough on the board. Dust the top with flour. Roll again, in the same direction as before, to a thickness of $1/2''$. Fold again into thirds.

Wrap in wax paper and refrigerate. Place in the freezer if you want to use it right away. When chilled, cut off about $1/3$ for each 9″ pie. Roll out (again, in the same direction). The dough is even better if refrigerated again after lining the pie dish. In this case, refrigerate until the filling is added. Once rolled, and lining a pie plate, the dough may be sealed and frozen.

MAKING A LATTICE TOP

To make a lattice top, roll out the dough to be used. Take a pie dish that is the same size as the one to be used. Place this pie dish on the dough, rim side down. Cut the dough around the edge of the pie dish, making a circle.

Cut the dough into narrow strips of equal width. The strips may be left flat or twisted end-to-end. Place half of the strips in one direction across the pie. Place the longest strips in the middle. Weave the remaining strips evenly through the first strips. Again, use the longest strips in the middle. Wet the ends of the strips lightly with water and crimp to the edges of the bottom crust.

APRICOT GLAZE

Use this glaze as a waterproofing for pie crusts. Once made, keep refrigerated.

1 cup apricot preserves
1 tablespoon sugar
3 tablespoons apricot brandy

Warm the preserves and the sugar in a double boiler until they begin to liquify. Press through a strainer to eliminate the pieces of apricot. Stir in the brandy.

To keep, refrigerate in a tightly capped jar. Warm the apricot glaze before using.

Use the leftover apricot pieces in **DEEP-DISH APPLE PIE** or **SUMMER FRUIT TARTS.**

CHERRY PIE

1 pie pastry
3 cups sour cherries
$1/3$ cup sugar (less if the
    cherries are sweet)
$1^1/_2$ tablespoons all-purpose
    flour
1 egg
$2/3$ cup cream
1 teaspoon sugar

Preheat oven to 450°.

Line one 9″ pie plate with pastry.

Wash and drain the cherries. If you are using frozen cherries, pour into a bowl without defrosting. Measure the sugar and flour and mix well. Stir into the cherries until they are well covered. Pour into the uncooked pie pastry. Bake at 450° for 10 minutes. Reduce heat to 350° and bake for 45 minutes.

Just before the 45 minutes are up, beat the egg until light. Stir the cream and sugar into the egg. Remove the pie from the oven and pour the egg-cream mixture over the top. Bake for 10 minutes, or until the custard is set.

Makes one 9″ pie.

RHUBARB-RAISIN PIE

This pie also is very good with a mixture of half rhubarb and half strawberries. However, as the strawberries tend to be sweeter, cut down on the amount of sugar added.

1 pie pastry with lattice top
3 cups fresh or frozen
   rhubarb, chopped
1 cup raisins
$1/3$ cup sugar (less if the
   rhubarb is sweet)
1 tablespoon cornstarch
$1/4$ teaspoon cinnamon
$1/2$ tablespoon water
1 tablespoon butter
Cream

Preheat oven to 450°.

Line an 8″ pie plate with the pastry. Mix the fruit with the water. Combine the sugar, cornstarch, and cinnamon and add to the fruit and the water. Mix well and pour into the pie pastry. Cut the butter into small pieces and dot the top. Cover with a lattice top, and brush with a few drops of cream.

Bake at 450° for 10 minutes. Reduce heat to 350°. Bake 35 minutes longer.

Makes one 8″ pie.

PEACH PIE

1 pie pastry
APRICOT GLAZE or 1 egg white
4 cups peaches, sliced
4 tablespoons all-purpose
   flour
¼ teaspoon salt
¾ cup sugar
¼ teaspoon cinnamon
¼ teaspoon nutmeg
1 cup cream
1 teaspoon lemon juice
1 tablespoon brown sugar
¼ teaspoon cinnamon

Preheat oven to 400°.

Line a 9½″ pie plate with pastry and brush with apricot glaze or with the white of an egg mixed with a little water. Fill with the sliced peaches.

In a small bowl, mix the flour, salt, sugar, cinnamon, and

nutmeg. Stir in the cream and the lemon juice. Pour over the peaches. Sprinkle the brown sugar mixed with the cinnamon over the top. Bake for 50-60 minutes.

Makes one 9^1/$_2$" pie.

GREEN PEAR PIE

This pie is made with Anjou pears. Any type of pear will do, although we prefer pears that are firm and near-ripe. When used in pies, such pears retain their distinctive texture and the fruit is not reduced to a characterless mush.

1 pie pastry with lattice
APRICOT GLAZE or 1 egg
    white
5 large Anjou pears (or any
    firm, near-ripe pears)
^{2}/$_3$ cup sugar
1-2 tablespoons all-purpose
    flour
1^1/$_2$ tablespoons butter
Juice of 1 lemon
Cinnamon

Line a deep-dish 9" pie plate with the pastry. Roll out and cut the strips for the lattice top. Refrigerate both until needed.

Peel and slice the pears. Remove the pie plate from the refrigerator. Brush the pastry with apricot glaze or with the white of 1 egg. Mix the sugar and 1-2 tablespoons flour, depending on how juicy your pears are.

Preheat oven to 425°.

Line the pastry with a layer of pears. Sprinkle with the sugar-flour mixture, then with some of the lemon juice. Dot with bits of butter. Continue in this fashion until all ingredients have been used. Sprinkle the last layer with cinnamon.

Arrange the dough strips to form a lattice top. Bake for 10 minutes. Reduce heat to 350° and bake for 50 minutes.

Makes one 9″ deep-dish pie.

DEEP-DISH APPLE PIE

As you prepare this, you will find the apples rising well above the rim of the pie plate. However, do not use fewer apples. The apples will fall considerably in baking.

1 double pie pastry
4 pounds tart apples
2 teaspoons cinnamon
$1/2$ cup brown sugar, firmly
   packed
2 teaspoons flour
$1/2$ cup apricot preserves
APRICOT GLAZE or 1 egg
   white
1 tablespoon butter
3 tablespoons brandy

Line a 9″ deep-dish pie plate with the bottom pastry. Roll out the top pastry to about twice the thickness of the bottom pastry. Keep this separate. Refrigerate both until ready to use.

Peel the apples and slice them into a large bowl. Mix the cinnamon, sugar, and flour. Warm the apricot preserves in a small saucepan until they begin to liquify.

Preheat oven to 425°.

Remove the pie plate from the refrigerator. Brush with apricot glaze or the white of 1 egg mixed with a little water. Line the pastry first with a layer of apples. Sprinkle with some of the sugar-cinnamon-flour mixture. Spoon some of the preserves over this. Continue in this fashion until all of the ingredients have been used. Dot with bits of the butter.

Cover with the upper pastry. Pinch the edges well, moistening with a little water, if necessary. With a knife, make four small holes in the center.

Bake at 425° for 10 minutes.

Reduce heat to 350° and bake for 40 minutes.

When the pie is done, remove from oven. Carefully spoon the brandy through the holes in the top. Serve hot.

Makes one 9″ deep-dish pie.

SUMMER FRUIT TARTS

This is a "free-form" recipe. The quantities will depend on the number of tarts you will be making. The sugar is sprinkled more liberally on the fruit that is most tart (lemon slices, for example). The fruit may be arranged in any combination. However, after several experiments, we have always returned to the order given below, finding it to be best.

Unusual and tangy, this is a tart that should be eaten only while hot. If you have apricots left over from making **APRICOT GLAZE**, these may be added. If you do this, omit some of the sugar.

Tart pans lined with pie
   pastry
Pastry for lattice tops
APRICOT GLAZE or 1 egg
   white
Bananas, sliced
Lemon slices, peeled
Orange slices, peeled
Pineapple slices, peeled
Pecans, chopped
Brown sugar
Butter
Cream

Line the tart pans with pastry and refrigerate. Reserve dough for the lattice top and refrigerate, as well. Just before using, brush the pastry with the apricot glaze or a lightly beaten egg white.

Prepare the fruit, saving the juice.

Preheat oven to 450°.

Layer the tart pans with the fruit in the order given above, sprinkling sugar over each layer. Dot the pineapple with bits of butter. Sprinkle with the pecans. Pour some of the reserved juice into each tart. Arrange the pieces for the lattice top. Crimp well. Brush with an apricot glaze (or a little cream). Bake for 10 minutes at 450°.

Reduce heat to 350°.

Bake for 20 minutes. Serve hot.

BANANA PIE

Molasses gives this pie a rich brown color. However, if you prefer, 1 tablespoon of honey may be substituted for the molasses.

1 pie pastry
1 cup bananas, mashed
   (about 2 medium bananas)
$^1\!/_2$ cup sugar
2 tablespoons molasses
$^1\!/_2$ teaspoon salt
1 egg
1 teaspoon cinnamon
$^1\!/_2$ teaspoon allspice
$^1\!/_2$ cup milk
$^1\!/_3$ cup cream

Preheat the oven to 400°.

Line a 9″ pie plate with pastry and chill well. Add the sugar, molasses (or honey), and salt to the mashed bananas. Beat the egg well and add. Stir in the spices, milk, and cream. Pour into the chilled crust. Bake for 5 minutes.

Reduce heat to 325°. Bake for 35 minutes, or until firm.

Makes one 9″ pie.

COCOANUT CUSTARD PIE

If you are fortunate enough to have fresh cocoanut, substitute 1 cup of cocoanut milk for 1 cup of milk. Grate the cocoanut meat over the top of the pie just before baking.

1 pie pastry
3 eggs
$1/_3$ cup sugar
2 cups milk
1 teaspoon creme de cacao
    (or 1 teaspoon vanilla)
Flaked cocoanut

Preheat oven to 325°.

Line one 9″ pie plate with pastry. Chill well. Beat the eggs well. Add the sugar, milk, and creme de cacao.

Pour into the chilled pastry. Sprinkle the cocoanut liberally over the surface.

Bake for 35-40 minutes, or until the custard is firm and lightly browned.

Makes one 9″ pie.

NUTMEG CUSTARD

4 cups milk
8 egg yolks
5 teaspoons sugar
$^1/_4$ teaspoon salt
2 teaspoons vanilla
nutmeg

Preheat oven to 300°.

Scald the milk. Beat the egg yolks until light, and add the sugar and salt. Slowly beat in the scalded milk, a little at a time, until all is used. Add the vanilla.

Pour into custard cups and sprinkle with nutmeg. Place cups in a pan of water and bake 20-30 minutes. The custard is done when a knife blade inserted at the edge comes out clean.

Makes about 10 servings.

Cakes

SPONGE CAKE

1 cup cake flour, sifted
$^1/_4$ teaspoon salt
2 tablespoons lemon juice (or
   $^1/_2$ lemon, juice and grated
   rind)
1 cup sugar
5 eggs

Resift the flour, adding the salt. Grate the lemon rind and add to the sugar.

Preheat oven to 325°.

Beat the egg yolks until thick and light in color. Gradually beat in the sugar and the grated rind. Add the lemon juice.

With a whisk, beat the egg whites until firm (but not dry). Fold half of these into the yolk mixture. Fold in the flour and salt. Fold in the remaining egg whites. Bake in an ungreased 10″ tube pan for 1 hour. Invert pan for 1 hour to cool before removing cake.

If you are using this for a pineapple upside-down cake, pour the batter onto the pineapple slices and bake *1 hour*. If desired, substitute 2 tablespoons pineapple juice for the lemon juice.

Makes one 10″ tube cake.

EVERYONE'S FAVORITE— ANGEL FOOD CAKE

The use of a wire whisk, rather than an electric mixer, will ensure the goodness of this cake. The use of a wire whisk does not add much in time or effort, but makes all the difference in the success of your angel food cake. Besides, it's fun! For the use of leftover egg yolks, see **GOLD CAKE CUPCAKES.**

1¼ cups egg whites
1 cup cake flour, sifted
1½ cups sugar
¼ teaspoon salt
1 teaspoon cream of tartar
1 teaspoon vanilla
¼ teaspoon almond extract

Preheat oven to 300°.

Separate the eggs. Let the whites set out until they reach room temperature. Resift the flour, adding one-half of the sugar. Resift the flour and sugar two more times.

Put the egg whites into a large bowl and add the salt. Beat with a wire whisk until foamy. Add the cream of tartar. Continue to beat until the whisk leaves a faint line when drawn through the egg whites. Beat in the remaining sugar a tablespoon at a time. Continue to beat until the mixture will hold in soft peaks. Add the vanilla and the almond extract.

Gradually sift the flour over the mixture and fold it in gently but thoroughly after each addition. Pour into an ungreased 10" tube pan and bake for 1 hour. Remove from the oven and invert the cake pan. Cool for about 1½ hours before removing.

Makes one 10" tube cake.

PINEAPPLE UPSIDE-DOWN CAKE

This is a short-cut recipe for a last-minute dessert. However, for a superior-tasting cake, substitute **SPONGE CAKE** for the batter and bake at 325° for 1 hour. You will not be disappointed.

¹/₂ cup butter
1 cup brown sugar, firmly
   packed
5-6 slices pineapple, drained

Melt the butter in a heavy 10″ round iron skillet, 3″ deep. Add the brown sugar and spread evenly over the bottom. Place the drained pineapple slices on top.

CAKE BATTER

¹/₄ cup pineapple juice (or
   other juice, or water)
3 eggs
³/₄ cup sugar
1 cup cake flour, sifted
1 teaspoon baking powder
¹/₄ teaspoon salt
¹/₂ teaspoon vanilla

Preheat oven to 300°.

Add the juice to the eggs and beat well. Beat in the sugar gradually until the mixture is thick and light-lemon colored.

Resift the flour and add the baking powder and salt. Add to the batter and beat only until blended. Add the vanilla. Pour into the skillet and bake for 30 minutes.

Remove from the oven. Turn upside-down on a platter. When cool, serve with whipped cream.

Makes one 10″ round cake.

OLD-FASHIONED WHITE CAKE

This recipe makes a large cake and is quite simple to prepare. Use the leftover yolks for **GOLD CAKE CUPCAKES** or **RICH POUND CAKE.** Recipe may easily be doubled.

1 cup butter
2 cups sugar
1 teaspoon vanilla (or ¹/₄
    teaspoon almond extract)
1 cup milk
3¹/₄ cups cake flour, sifted
3¹/₂ teaspoons baking powder
8 egg whites

Preheat oven to 275°.

Grease a 14″ x 10″ x 2″ dish (or three 8″ round cake pans). Cream the butter and sugar. Add the vanilla or the almond extract to the milk. Resift the flour and baking powder. Alternate adding the dry and liquid ingredients to the creamed butter and sugar. Beat the egg whites until stiff, not dry, and fold them into the batter. Bake for 45 minutes.

Makes one 14″ x 10″ x 2″ cake, or three 8″ round cakes.

COCOA FROSTING

$^1/_2$ cup butter
6 tablespoons cream
4 heaping tablespoons cocoa
4 cups confectioners' sugar
1 teaspoon very strong coffee

Melt the butter. Add the cream and cocoa. Bring to a boil, stirring constantly. Stir in the sugar, then the coffee. Spread on the warm cake.

CHECKERBOARD CAKE

1 teaspoon instant coffee,
   ground to a powder
1 teaspoon ground cloves
1 teaspoon cinnamon
$^1/_2$ teaspoon black pepper
$3^1/_3$ cups cake flour, sifted
$3^3/_4$ teaspoons baking powder
$^2/_3$ cup butter (about 11
   tablespoons)
2 cups sugar
3 eggs
1 cup milk
3 tablespoons molasses
$^1/_2$ cup raisins

Grease a 14" x 10" x 2" dish. Using the back of a spoon, grind the coffee into a powder. Measure and mix in the cloves, cinnamon, and black pepper. Resift the flour, adding the baking powder. Cream the butter and sugar in a large bowl. Separate the eggs, placing the whites in another large bowl. Add the yolks, one at a time, to the creamed butter and sugar. Alternate adding the flour and milk until all is well mixed.

Preheat oven to 300°.

Beat the egg whites until stiff and fold in.

Divide the batter between both bowls. Into one, stir in the powdered coffee, spices, molasses, and raisins.

Pour a line of light batter lengthwise into the dish, smoothing with a spatula. Next to it pour a line of dark batter, then another line of light. Use only half of each batter and smooth with a spatula.

Start again, this time with the dark batter (over the light); then the light. End with the dark, using all of the remaining batter. Bake for 50 minutes.

Makes one 14″ x 10″ x 2″ cake.

No matter how many times you make this cake, you will always have the feeling that the divisions might have been better. There is no need to worry, because it always turns out fine. The batter may be poured into any design or pattern.

GOLD CAKE CUPCAKES

This recipe is a good one for leftover egg yolks. (It can also be used to make a gold cake. Time and pan size are the same as for **OLD-FASHIONED WHITE CAKE**).

2 cups sugar
8 egg yolks
1 cup butter
$^1/_2$ teaspoon almond extract
1 cup milk
$3^1/_3$ cups cake flour, sifted
$3^1/_2$ teaspoons baking powder
1 cup chopped dates
    (optional)

Preheat oven to 275°.

Line, or grease the cupcake tins. Cream the sugar and egg yolks. Cream in the butter. Add the almond extract to the milk. Resift the flour with the baking powder.

Alternate adding the flour and the milk to the sugar, egg yolks, and butter mixture. Stir in the dates. Pour into the cupcake tins and bake for 20 minutes.

Makes 36 cupcakes.

BILL'S FLYING CHOCOLATE CAKE

$^3/_4$ cup unsweetened
    chocolate, grated (or about
    $2^1/_3$ oz.)
$^1/_2$ cup milk
$^2/_3$ cup dark brown sugar
1 egg yolk

Put all of the above into a double boiler. Cook until the chocolate is melted and the mixture is thick enough to coat the spoon (about 5-10 minutes). Remove from the heat and cool, stirring for the first few minutes.

CAKE BATTER

$^1/_2$ cup butter
1 cup dark brown sugar
2 eggs
$2^1/_2$ cups cake flour, sifted
$^1/_2$ cup milk
1 teaspoon vanilla
1 teaspoon baking soda
1 teaspoon warm water

Preheat oven to 275°.

Grease two 9″ round cake pans. Cream the butter and sugar and add the eggs, one at a time. Resift the flour, and alternate adding it with the milk. Stir in the chocolate mixture by hand and blend thoroughly. Add the vanilla. Dissolve the baking soda in a teaspoonful of warm water and add. Mix thoroughly and pour into the two cake pans. Bake for 30 minutes. Remove from the oven and let stand for about 5 minutes. Remove from pans and place right-side-up on racks to cool.

Makes two 9″ round cakes.

CARAMEL FROSTING

$^1/_2$ cup butter
$^1/_4$ cup milk
1 cup brown sugar, firmly packed
1 $^3/_4$-2 cups confectioners' sugar

Melt the butter in a saucepan and stir in the brown sugar. Bring to a boil. Stir in the milk and continue to stir until mixture has reached a boil. Cool. Add the confectioners' sugar, beating well after each addition.

MOLASSES CAKE

This freezes well and is quite moist.

2 cups all-purpose flour,
   sifted
$^1/_2$ teaspoon powdered cloves
$^1/_2$ teaspoon cinnamon
$^1/_2$ teaspoon allspice
$^1/_2$ teaspoon nutmeg
1 teaspoon baking soda
$^1/_2$ cup butter
$^1/_2$ cup molasses
2 eggs
$^1/_2$ cup milk
1 cup raisins

Preheat oven to 300°.

Grease a 9″ round cake pan. Resift the flour, adding the cloves, cinnamon, allspice, nutmeg, and soda. Set aside. Cream the butter and molasses. Add the eggs and beat well.

Alternate adding the flour mixture and the milk to the molasses mixture. Stir in the raisins. Bake for 30 minutes.

Makes one 9″ round cake.

PEACH KUCHEN

This is definitely a favorite. This recipe may be halved to fill an 8″ square dish. If this is done, the first time in the oven may take only 15 minutes (or until the sugar mixture begins to bubble). Pour the sugar evenly. Be certain to pour it around the edges of the dish as this helps to seal the bottom layer.

4 cups all-purpose flour,
   sifted
$^1/_2$ teaspoon baking powder
1 teaspoon salt
2 cups sugar
1 cup butter
A 1 pound 13 ounce-can of
   peach halves, drained
A 1 pound-can of peach
   slices, drained
2 teaspoons cinnamon
1 teaspoon nutmeg
4 egg yolks, beaten
2 cups whipping cream

Preheat oven to 450°.

Grease a 9″ x 13″ dish. Resift the flour with the baking powder, salt, and 4 tablespoons of the sugar. Cut in the butter until all is the consistency of cornmeal.

Place the crumb mixture in the dish and press lightly and evenly. Over this, arrange the peach halves, then the peach slices. Mix the remaining sugar with the cinnamon and nutmeg and sprinkle over the peaches. Be careful to cover all the edges of the dish.

Bake for 20 minutes. Mix the beaten egg yolks and cream. Remove the dish from the oven and pour the egg and cream mixture over the top. Bake for 15 minutes longer, or until custard is set.

Makes one 9″ x 13″ kuchen.

COTTAGE CHEESECAKE

All cheesecakes will shrink somewhat after cooking. To lessen this shrinkage, open the oven door slightly and allow the cake to cool in the oven. This cake will be a rich brown on top.

1 pound (2 cups) cottage
　　cheese
1 cup sugar
2 tablespoons all-purpose
　　flour
$2^1/_2$ tablespoons lemon juice
　　(or juice and grated rind of
　　lemon)
4 eggs
1 cup cream
$^1/_4$ teaspoon salt

CRUMB CRUST

2 cups zwieback crumbs
$^1/_3$ cup butter, melted
1 tablespoon sugar

Combine and mix well until the mixture holds together. Press into a 10″ springform pan and around sides.

Preheat oven to 400°.

Press the cottage cheese through a fine sieve and cream until smooth. Add the sugar, flour, and lemon juice and rind. Separate the eggs; beat the yolks slightly and add to the cottage cheese. Add the cream and mix well.

Add salt to the egg whites. Beat with a whisk until firm but not dry. Fold in gently, but thoroughly. Pour batter into crumb-lined pan. Bake at 400° for 5 minutes; then at 325° for 1 hour, or until firm.

Makes one 10″ round cake.

DATE-NUT CAKE

1½ cups chopped dates
1 cup boiling water
½ cup butter
1 cup sugar
1 egg
1⅔ cups cake flour, sifted
1 teaspoon baking soda
½ teaspoon salt
1 teaspoon vanilla
½ cup chopped nuts

Preheat oven to 300°.

Grease an 8″ square dish. In a saucepan, mix the dates with the boiling water and cool to lukewarm. Cream the butter and sugar and add the egg. Blend in the date mixture. Resift the flour, adding the baking soda and salt. Beat into the batter. Add the vanilla and stir in the chopped nuts. Bake for 45-50 minutes.

Makes one 8″ square cake.

RICH POUND CAKE

3¹/₃ cups cake flour, sifted
1 teaspoon salt
¹/₄ teaspoon baking soda
¹/₂ teaspoon mace
1 cup butter
3 cups sugar
6 eggs
1 teaspoon vanilla
¹/₂ pint sour cream

Preheat oven to 250°.

Grease a 10″ tube pan. Resift the flour, adding the salt, baking soda, and mace. Cream the butter and the sugar. Add the eggs, one at a time, mixing well after each.

Mix the vanilla with the sour cream. Alternate adding this and the flour mixture to the shortening, sugar, and eggs. Pour into the tube pan and bake for 1 hour and 45 minutes.

Makes one 10″ tube cake.

NUTTY BANANA CAKE

$\frac{1}{2}$ cup butter
1$\frac{1}{2}$ cups sugar
2 eggs
1$\frac{3}{4}$ cups cake flour, sifted
$\frac{1}{2}$ teaspoon baking powder
$\frac{1}{2}$ teaspoon baking soda
$\frac{1}{2}$ teaspoon salt
$\frac{1}{4}$ cup buttermilk
1 teaspoon vanilla
1 cup ripe mashed bananas
    (2 or 3)
$\frac{3}{4}$ cup chopped walnuts

Preheat oven to 300°.

Grease a 9″ x 13″ dish. Cream the butter and sugar. Beat in the eggs, one at a time. Resift the flour, adding the baking powder, baking soda, and salt. Alternate adding it with the buttermilk. Add the vanilla, then the bananas and nuts. Pour into the greased dish and bake for 40 minutes.

Makes one 9″ x 13″ cake.

Cookies

MOIST PUMPKIN COOKIES

2/3 cup butter
   (approximately 11
   tablespoons)
1 1/2 cups brown sugar
2 eggs
1 16-ounce can pumpkin
3 cups all-purpose flour,
   sifted
1/2 teaspoon salt
1/2 teaspoon ginger
3/4 teaspoon cinnamon
3/4 teaspoon nutmeg
1/2 teaspoon allspice
4 1/2 teaspoons baking powder
1 1/4 teaspoons lemon juice
1 1/4 cups raisins
1 1/4 cups chopped nuts

Preheat oven to 325°.

Cream the butter and the brown sugar. Add the eggs, one at a time. Add the pumpkin. Resift the flour, adding the spices and baking powder. Add to the pumpkin mixture, mixing well. Add the lemon juice. Stir in the raisins and the chopped nuts. Spoon drop onto cookie sheets and bake for 15-18 minutes.

Makes 75 cookies.

GRANDMA'S PEANUT BUTTER COOKIES

$^1/_2$ cup brown sugar
$^1/_2$ cup white sugar
$^1/_2$ cup peanut butter
1 egg
$^1/_2$ cup milk
$^1/_2$ teaspoon vanilla
1$^1/_2$ cup all-purpose flour,
   sifted
1 teaspoon baking soda
$^1/_8$ teaspoon salt

Preheat oven to 325°.

Cream the two sugars and the peanut butter. Add the egg, then the milk. Beat well. Resift the flour, adding the baking soda and the salt. Add to the mixture gradually, mixing well. Drop from a spoon onto an ungreased cookie sheet and bake for 12 minutes.

Makes about 18 large cookies.

SAND TARTS

To avoid frustration, make sure the dough is well chilled before attempting to roll out.

$^1/_2$ cup butter
$^1/_2$ cup sugar
1 egg
1$^1/_2$ cup all-purpose flour,
   sifted
Sugar or chopped nuts

Cream the butter and sugar. Separate the egg, and add the yolk. Resift the flour and add. Refrigerate the dough for 40 minutes.

Preheat oven to 300°.

Roll dough quickly, and as thin as possible on a well-floured board. Cut out cookies with a 3″ biscuit or cookie cutter and place on a cookie sheet. Brush with the egg white and sprinkle with sugar or chopped nuts. Bake for 15 minutes.

Makes about 2 dozen cookies.

GINGER COOKIES

This recipe has survived generations of discriminating ginger cookie lovers.

1 cup butter
2 cups sugar
2 eggs
$^1/_2$ cup molasses
4 cups all-purpose flour,
    sifted
3 teaspoons cinnamon
4 teaspoons ginger
2 teaspoons baking soda
1 teaspoon salt

Cream the butter and sugar. Add the eggs one at a time, then the molasses. Resift the flour, adding the spices, baking soda, and salt. Add and mix well. Chill the dough several hours.

Preheat oven to 300°.

Roll dough into small balls and dust with sugar, if desired. Place on ungreased cookie sheet and bake for 15 minutes.

Makes 70 cookies.

DATE-FILLED COOKIES

Our favorites! And they look as good as they taste.

FILLING
$\frac{1}{3}$ cup boiling water
$\frac{3}{4}$ cup dates, pitted and
    sliced
$\frac{1}{4}$ cup honey
$\frac{1}{2}$ tablespoon lemon juice
$\frac{1}{2}$ tablespoon butter
DOUGH
$1\frac{3}{4}$ cups all-purpose flour,
    sifted
$1\frac{1}{2}$ teaspoons baking powder
$\frac{1}{4}$ teaspoon salt
$\frac{1}{8}$ cup honey
$\frac{1}{3}$ cup butter
1 egg
$\frac{1}{2}$ teaspoon vanilla
$\frac{1}{4}$ cup milk
$\frac{1}{2}$ cup chopped nuts

Boil the water in a small saucepan. Add the dates and boil for about 5 minutes. Add the $\frac{1}{4}$ cup honey, $\frac{1}{2}$ tablespoon lemon juice, and $\frac{1}{2}$ tablespoon butter. Set aside to cool.

Resift the flour, adding the baking powder and the salt. Cream the honey and the butter in a medium bowl. Add the egg and the vanilla. Alternate adding the dry ingredients and milk.

Refrigerate both the date mixture and the dough until thoroughly chilled. Or, (if in a hurry) put in the freezer to chill.

When the dough is chilled and firm, preheat oven to 325°.

Roll the dough out on a lightly floured board to a thickness of about 1/8″. Cut out all the pieces with a 3″ biscuit cutter. Stir the nuts into the date filling. Using only half of the cut-out pieces, drop the date-nut mixture into the middle of each one. The mixture may be liberally spread, but must never be allowed to touch the edges. Cover with the remaining half of the cut-out pieces. Crimp the edges firmly together with the tines of a fork or a dough crimper. Place on a cookie sheet and bake immediately for 15 minutes.

Makes 1 dozen cookies.

GRAHAM WAFERS

These are little more than oversized graham crackers. But they are fun on picnics, and who doesn't like grahams and a glass of milk?

1/2 cup butter
1/2 cup sugar
3 cups graham flour
1/2 teaspoon baking soda
1/2 cup milk

Preheat oven to 300°.

Cream the butter and sugar. Mix the graham flour and baking

soda. Alternate adding the flour and the milk until all are mixed. Roll out on a floured board and cut with a biscuit cutter to any size or shape desired. Place on a cookie sheet and bake for 20 minutes.

Makes 25 large graham wafers.

SOFT SUGAR COOKIES

For those who enjoy nibbling the batter as much as eating the finished product, beware! This is quite rich. The dough may be refrigerated for a couple of days, if desired.

1 cup butter
2 cups sugar
3 eggs
1 teaspoon baking soda
1 cup sour cream
4 cups all-purpose flour,
    sifted
1 teaspoon vanilla
Cinnamon
1 cup raisins (optional)
1 cup chopped nuts
    (optional)

Preheat oven to 300°.

Cream the butter and sugar. Add the eggs one at a time, beating well after each addition. Dissolve the soda in the sour cream and add to the mixture. Resift the flour and add, beating well. Add the vanilla. Stir in raisins and/or nuts. Spoon out onto an ungreased cookie sheet. Dot with cinnamon or a cinnamon-/sugar mixture, if preferred. Bake for about 15-20 minutes.

Makes about 60 good-sized cookies.

CRUMPIES

A little bit of everything. Good for lunches.

$^1/_2$ cup butter
$^1/_2$ cup white sugar
$^1/_2$ cup brown sugar
1 egg
$^1/_2$ teaspoon vanilla
1 cup all-purpose flour, sifted
$^1/_2$ teaspoon baking soda
$^1/_4$ teaspoon salt
1 cup uncooked wheat bran
1 cup rolled oats
$^1/_2$ cup coconut

Preheat oven to 300°.

Cream the butter and sugars. Add the egg and mix well. Add the vanilla. Resift the flour with the baking soda and salt and add. Stir in the bran, oats, and coconut. Mix well. Spoon onto an ungreased cookie sheet and bake 8-10 minutes.

Makes approximately 3 dozen crumpies.

RAISIN-OATMEALS

To double this recipe, use ³/₄ cup butter, 2 cups oatmeal, and 3 eggs.

5¹/₂ tablespoons butter
¹/₂ cup sugar
1 cup all-purpose flour, sifted
¹/₂ teaspoon cinnamon
¹/₈ teaspoon salt
¹/₄ teaspoon baking soda
1¹/₄ cups oatmeal
2 eggs
¹/₂ cup raisins

Preheat oven to 300°.

Grease a cookie sheet. Cream the butter and sugar. Resift the flour, adding the cinnamon, salt, and baking soda. Add to the creamed sugar and butter. Mix well. Add the oatmeal and mix thoroughly. Add the eggs one at a time. Stir in the raisins. Spoon out onto the cookie sheet and bake for 20 minutes.

Makes 2 dozen cookies.

Index